Steve Kenning is a
'Positivity' is a de
style.

If you haven't read
know Detective ..... .с.ии of the
wonderful city of Barcelona.

Here are some of the words written about the books of Steve Kenning:

'If you love Barcelona and you love reading fiction the chances are that you have spent a frustrating time searching for modern day fiction based in the city. Apart from Montalban, there is very little based in modern day Barcelona. Now though, there is a new Barcelona thriller writer on the scene, Steve Kenning.'

Barcelona Reporter

'A pacy thriller, that introduces readers to the delights of Barcelona.'

Evening Herald

'The book reflects very well the current atmosphere of Barcelona.'

Roma Bosch

Steve Kenning

Other books by Steve Kenning:

Thrillers:

La Hermandad del Noveno Noviembre
(The Brotherhood of the Ninth November)
– *introducing Detective Will Ferran*

Barcelona Betrayal
-A Detective Will Ferran thriller

Positivity

Acknowledgements

This book was written partly as a response to the repeated interested conversations I had with a wide range of people relating to the management and leadership style I have developed over the years. As a result of this interest I felt the need to put down my thoughts on life and how to live it. I thank these people for their interest, their conversation and their support.

Another reason for writing this book was to try to help other people find the joy that I am lucky enough to have in my life. My father died recently and I remember him very fondly, I miss him but most of all I am very grateful for the happy and positive genes he and my mother have passed on to me. My life is completed by the two delightful children I have and my best friend, and inspiration, my lovely wife Paula.

Thanks also to all the people mentioned in this book, I've changed your names to protect your anonymity, but you know who you are. I have learnt from you all. Thank you!

Steve Kenning

First published 2007

Copyright © Steve Kenning 2006

Pensadores Futuros

www.barca-only.com

British Library Cataloguing In Publication Data
A Record of this Publication is available
from the British Library

ISBN 1846855241
978-1-84685-524-5

First Published 2007 by

Exposure Publishing, an imprint of Diggory Press,
Three Rivers, Minions, Liskeard,
Cornwall, PL14 5LE, UK
WWW.DIGGORYPRESS.COM

STEVE KENNING

POSITIVITY

The Art of Personal Mastery

A Handbook to Inspire

Steve Kenning

Annoyingly *Positive* Statements:

'Footprints on the sands of time are never made by sitting down.'

'Remember that the door to opportunity swings two ways – in and out!'

'When you see a problem or an obstacle, always look upon it as a challenge.'

'You cannot discover new oceans unless you have the courage to lose sight of the shore.'

'It's never too late to become what you might have been.'

'Drifting through life without aim or purpose is the first cause of failure.'

'Today is the yesterday you worried about tomorrow.'

'You only learn how to succeed by failing, and no success is possible without it.'

How do you feel after reading these annoyingly positive statements?

Positivity

If you feel physically sick or really annoyed by any kind of positivity then you would be best advised to continue with your miserable, daily existence until you die. Perhaps you could read something like 'Gormenghast'* instead to bring some brightness and joy into your life!

However,

If you feel moderately annoyed yet you can sense a tingling of interest inside you, then perhaps you can be saved. Read on, who knows how your life may change as a result of reading this chunk of philosophy about modern day life.

But,

If you loved these quotes, definitely read on. This book will make you feel even better about yourself and possibly even give you a few tips on how to become even more positive and enlightened!

('Gormenghast' – a novel by Mervyn Peake - very dark and depressing).

What is life all about?

Or

What use is this book?

The greatest question ever, has to be - 'what is the meaning of life'?

Every one of us thinks about this question at some point in life and yet no one really knows the answer. The book 'The Hitchhiker's Guide to the Galaxy', by Douglas Adams, gives the answer as 42. This is probably as close as we will ever get to knowing the real answer. Perhaps though there is no meaning to life. If this is the case, why not put all your efforts into enjoying yourself and just do your best to help others enjoy themselves too.

This book is designed to be a source of inspiration, good quotes, interesting stories and sound advice. It is usually best not to give advice, but then you don't have to take any notice of it do you?

This book is essentially about dreams becoming reality – develop your dreams and develop the tools to help you to reach them.

Life is a journey – we need to enjoy the journey in every respect. Our dreams often translate into, essentially, aspirations.

Positivity

This book charts a course to creating aspirations in everyone. It is not a book that provides all the answers, far from it. It is a book to stimulate, to engender ideas and to encourage you, the reader, to take up the challenge to use aspirations as a vehicle for changing your life.

Use this book to:

- **Help** *manage your life* – it might make you realise that, as you only live once and could die at anytime, if you are going down the wrong track then maybe it's time you actually made some real decisions and made the most of your life. What would it take for you to enjoy yourself and become really happy?

- **Help** *run your company, team, or better manage your job.* If you actually look beyond the frivolity of this book you might find several sound pointers for making a success of your work life.

- **Help** *you live your dream.* C'mon, you know you really want to!

If we can engage, stimulate and challenge individual minds then perhaps we can really get the kind of individual achievement we all crave.

To do this we need to better understand the psychology and workings of individuals. We need to raise self-belief, self-esteem and above all create real aspirations in every individual. If people feel good about themselves and have aspirations they are more likely to achieve and more likely to be real, generative citizens. If people don't value themselves then nothing much matters.

Positivity

Contents *Page*

This doesn't exist in this book.

One of the aims of this book is to get you, the reader, to take more responsibility for your own life. So, if this book did have a contents page things would be just that little bit too easy for you. If you find something that you like in the book you will just have to find a suitable method for finding it again.

Have fun!

Steve Kenning

Background to this book

Or

The **reason** why I bothered to write this book

And

The basic philosophy behind it

One of the small pleasures I have in life, that make me smile inwardly, is when I meet someone and they ask me what I do for a job. I normally say I'm a teacher but if they push I tell them that I am in fact a Headteacher. Invariably they look a little taken aback. The reason for this is that I pride myself on not looking or behaving like everyone's stereotype of a Headteacher.

However, I have been a Headteacher of a very successful, large secondary school for a number of years and I meet many people in leadership positions who are not prepared to take that extra leap in thinking or extra risk to really make a difference to the people they lead and effect. People sometimes admire what we have achieved at my school but then often find every possible reason for not being able to implement similar things in their own organisations. This is not to say that what we are doing is necessarily the right way for everyone but at least we are trying to make a real difference.

Positivity

What we do at my school is not rocket science, but it is based on some very strong and well-embedded principles. Anyway, one core reason (REASON 1) to write this book is to share some of our proven principles and ideas with the hope that people might make some use of them to help them improve their life in some way.

So, this book is for anyone. I might be a Headteacher but I run an organisation with over 200 staff, 1300 students, more than 2000 parents and have dealings with hundreds of other people. In your daily life and in any organisation you have to deal with people. This book gives a few pointers as to how you might deal with people at any level to get the best out of them for the benefit of all.

> **'People just ain't no good**
> **I think that's well understood**
> **You can see it everywhere you look**
> **People just ain't no good'**
> *Nick Cave*

I think most of us would agree, at times, with the words of Nick Cave (who by the way is, in my view, a quite wonderful songwriter!). However, it is very easy to criticise others, to run them down, to be negative. It is much harder to look at people with a view to understanding them, to see inside them and to work out why they behave or act as they do. *Many people have fragile egos, low self-esteem, or low self-confidence.*

Steve Kenning

'Unfortunately, without really thinking, we sometimes, as leaders and teachers, destroy self-confidence in others by always looking for faults and being too negative. Too much energy is spent correcting faults instead of reinforcing what is good.'

Willy Railo from the book 'Sven Goran Ericksson'

TEST:

For the next 24 hours, rather than taking the easy option and having a good go at someone who annoys you, why not try to understand why they are saying what they are saying to you – have they got money problems, is their relationship on the edge, do they really envy you, do you make them feel small? – and try to help them to help themselves.

Just imagine how good you would feel if you could help just one person to feel better about themselves. ****For each person who would usually annoy you but, this time, you manage so you leave their company feeling positive, award yourself 5 points. For each person you actually make feel better about themselves, award yourself 10 points.*

Positivity

The technological human development programme.

The world is changing very, very rapidly at the moment. So fast that we don't even notice many of the changes – see what I mean, oh sorry you missed it.

SMART humans are those who can read the world and prepare themselves with the right skills and tools not only for survival, but also for success.

Just consider the technological human development programme so far:
- Ancient times – our main activity as humans was **trade**
- 1800's-1970's – our main activity as humans was **production** in an industrial society
- 1980's and 1990's – this was the **administrative** age in an information society
- Today – we are moving into a communication age in a very **creative** society

So today we have to develop ourselves creatively if we are to survive in the global economy. Already people are struggling to survive the new expectations of the workplace. The reasons for this are often due to:

- **An inability to focus on the task and lack of concentration to see it through**

- A tendency to be easily distracted and take things personally
- An inability to stand back and impartially consider their own performance and actions
- A predisposition to respond inappropriately to situations
- Low self-esteem and an unrealistic self-image or vision of where they are going in life

Francis Charters

Whether we like it or not the world has, and is, changing rapidly. You can accept it, embrace it and tool up for it or you can play the dinosaur, and we all know what a good strategy that is!

'We want our voices to be heard. We want control over our lives. This is a fundamental shift in social maturity that has been about five decades in the making, and is now having an explosive effect on the way we think of ourselves as citizens, as employees, as consumers.'

Soshana Zuboff, Professor of Business Administration, Harvard, 2004

Exactly!

Positivity

You may not even notice that you are becoming a stroppy, control freak, but we all are! So another reason for writing this book is to hopefully encourage people to understand themselves and the world a little more, and to become pro-active in the development of essential skills and tools for the world as it changes (REASON 2).

We need these competencies if people are to function effectively in life, work and society:
- Self awareness
- Self management
- Social awareness
- Relationship management

Of course, as this book is about trying to get you to help yourself feel better, enjoy yourself, and generally to like life, then health, both physical and mental health, also has to be seriously considered. We are all aware that there are a lot of strange people out there, with varying degrees of mental health. But mental health can affect anybody in a whole variety of forms from eating disorders to depression. So once again, if we can raise our personal feelgood factor, these mental health problems should be minimised.

Have you ever considered that?

- Health has no upper limit.
- As we develop technologically we are demanding medical improvements that slow

ageing and maximise beauty, wellbeing and performance.
- Health is being equated with the good life.
- Health is becoming a more important part of identity and lifestyle.

So this interest in health in the age of individualism means that your body is your own responsibility. You create your body yourself. The way we look can be perceived as a choice. The healthy human being is increasingly taking steps against ill health and risks.

I could say that another reason behind this book is that I want you to live to a grand old age, but as I don't know you, that would be a lie. But I do want this book to perhaps give you a kick, if you need one, to take some action and improve your mental and physical health (REASON 3).

The Central Philosophy : individual growth

'....basically today ....we generally have the basic needs to live......so we now need, first and foremost, to get self-worth'

Anne Skare Nielsen

In most developed economies today the vast majority of people have access to basic needs. You may disagree but it is true! So, what drives most people on, is very dependent on each individual, it

Positivity

could be money, power, fame, and all kinds of other motivators.

BUT all of us suffer, at some time, from a feeling of a lack of self-worth. *A casual comment from someone can destroy you if you are having a bad day - you might not get that job you wanted or perhaps not even an interview, your friends may seem to be ignoring you, or your relationship might have just broken up.* In a society such as ours, based on an emphasis on success and materialism, the amount of people with low self-worth or low self-esteem is a very real and growing problem. *People commit terrible crimes, not because they feel really good about themselves but because they don't care and don't value themselves.* **What does it feel like on a day when you feel great? You can achieve anything, nothing is beyond you.**

Just imagine what would happen to the economy, to crime figures, etc, if we all felt good about ourselves most of the time.

The central philosophy behind this book is to grow the individual person: individual growth. Because if we can satisfy the need for people:

- To understand themselves
- To recognise their strengths and weaknesses
- To see a value to self-improvement

Steve Kenning

.... Then their capacity for self-development should increase along with their feeling of self-worth.

Central to the philosophy of individual growth is the belief that we all have an unending potential to be better (or to improve ourselves).

Can you accept this statement?

There will always be people who say why do I want to get better, I'm happy with my life.

BUT ARE YOU REALLY?

Are you really happy with the way you speak to people at times? How do you feel about yourself? Are you really happy with your job?

TEST:

Make a list of all the things in your life that are so good you cannot imagine any of them getting any better than they already are.

**For each one on your list deduct five points – everything could be better, because even if you are sublimely happy, can you ensure it stays that way?

Positivity

When you can accept that we all have an unending potential to be better, then you have to learn to live these three objectives:

- Become your **UNIQUE** self. *There is no one in the world like you – respect yourself. You have a contribution to make which no one else can make.*

- Become **SELF-DIRECTED**. *You need to put yourself in the driving seat of your life and work.*

- Accept **ACCOUNTABILITY** for yourself and your actions. *Don't blame others for what happens to you.*

Individual growth is all about being in control of your own life - knowing yourself, taking action and taking responsibility.

A great book that explains all this in excellent and life-changing detail is 'The Fifth Discipline' by Peter Senge. He talks about personal mastery:

'People with a high level of personal mastery live in a continual learning mode. They never 'arrive".

He also says that:

'People with a high level of personal mastery are acutely aware of their ignorance, their incompetence, their growth areas. And they are deeply self-confident. Paradoxical?'

Peter Senge – The Fifth Discipline

The eight conditions for raising aspirations

With any philosophy you need a framework to give it direction and tools and strategies to make it happen. The tools and strategies will mostly come later but an excellent framework for helping each of us to raise our aspirations and to make the most of our life is this one:

> The eight conditions that affect aspirations:

- BELONGING is being accepted for who you are.
- HEROES are people who inspire your dreams.
- SENSE OF ACCOMPLISHMENT is how you feel being your best.
- FUN AND EXCITEMENT is simply making you smile.
- CURIOSITY AND CREATIVITY is allowing your mind to go anywhere at any time.

Positivity

- SPIRIT OF ADVENTURE is taking chances as reach for the stars.
- LEADERSHIP AND RESPONSIBILTY is doing what is right for others and yourself.
- CONFIDENCE TO TAKE ACTION is believing in yourself and doing something about it.

These 8 conditions are the result of a great amount of research over the past 15 years by Dr Russ Quaglia, Director of the Global Institute for Raising Student Aspirations, in Boston, USA (GISA). Although they are conditions central to raising aspirations in students they can be applied to anyone and any organisation.

What the 8 conditions provide is a framework or a checklist for you to take action. Do you feel a sense of belonging? If not, why not? Then investigate ways of making improvements and take action.

Chapter One

The RETURN OF THE JEDI

What do you really want to be like?

'**The greatest danger for most is not that our aim is too high and we miss it, but that our aim is too low and we reach it.**'
Michaelangelo

Some things just live in your mind. Who knows what impact they have on the choices and decisions you make. These things live in your sub-conscious but help shape who you are.

We are all very complex beings and the influences that have conditioned us are impossible to fully understand. However, certain key memories can be tracked back and their influence assessed.

STORY:

I must have seen the first 'Star Wars' film seven or eight times when it first came out and many more times since, and each time I loved the image of the Jedi. Sir Alec Guiness as Obe-Wan Kenobi (Ben) in particular is etched on my memory. The scene I really love from the film is when Ben and Luke are in Tatooine and are stopped by several

Positivity

stormtroopers. Luke is being questioned when Ben speaks to the storm-trooper in a very controlled voice:

Ben:	**'You don't need to see his identification.'**
Trooper:	**'We don't need to see his identification.'**
Ben:	**'These are not the droids you are looking for.'**
Trooper:	**'These are not the droids we are looking for.'**
Ben:	**'He can go about his business.'**
Trooper:	**'He can go about his business.'**

This level of coolness and control left a real mark on me. The image of a Jedi was, for me, quite aspirational!

Stimulus

As Jedi's don't really exist it was impossible for me to aspire to be one, however, it wasn't the physical aspect of being a Jedi that really attracted me – it was the qualities to which Jedi's aspired that I was drawn to. As a result I have tried to live my life, certainly as a leader, in accordance with qualities associated with being a Jedi. These qualities are all centred around the illumination, inner growth, and peace that comes from inner resolution and deepened understanding:

- **Selfless excellence**
  - *To seek excellence in all endeavors to the benefit of others rather than in personal aggrandizement.*
- **Fairness**
  - *Seek always the path of 'right', unencumbered by bias or personal interest.*
- **Loyalty**
  - *Be known for unwavering commitment to the people and ideals you choose to live by.*
- **Courage**
  - *Sometimes choosing the more difficult path, the personally expensive one.*
- **Faith**
  - *Have faith in your beliefs, for faith roots you and gives hope.*
- **Humility**
  - *Value first the contributions of others; do not boast of your own accomplishments, let others do this for you.*
- **Fearlessness**
  - *Fear leads to anger, anger leads to hate, and hate leads to suffering. The golden rule is to act fearlessly upon what one believes to be right.*

Positivity

- **Vision**
  - *Without a sound motive and purpose, action has no meaning, no destination, and lacks a foundation.*
- **Discipline**
  - *Ideally one's mind is a calm ocean, like a sea of glass.*
- **Focus**
  - *Focus on the moment, in the now, realizing that the stylus of time cuts in the present, and that history is perpetually in the making.*
- **Learning**
  - *Learning never ends. Remember that there is always something more to learn about.*
- **Integrity**
  - *Everyone has a responsibility to be honest with themselves.*

So aspiring to be like a Jedi is OK. After all a Jedi is really a person who knows themselves well and is there for other people.

Advice

If you really want to reach your aspirations, you need to spend a lot of time looking at yourself and your own behavior, attitudes, etc.

Steve Kenning

Self-knowledge is the starting point. *A period of real undisturbed reflection could change both your own life and, as a result, the lives of a lot of other people.*

Action point:

Decide what you want, what are your aspirations? Forget about what you might consider to be impossible. Consider the kind of person you want to be. **Over a few days find time for yourself. Reflect on your strengths, weaknesses and dreams.**

Inspiration:

- Liam Neeson, as a Jedi in Star Wars: The Phantom Menace.
  Was he cool, or what?

- Wilko Johnson (former lead guitarist of a band called Dr Feelgood).
  I really wanted to play guitar like Wilko, he was my inspiration!

- Charlie Aitken (the dependable, ever present Aston Villa left-back in the 1960's/1970's).
  Charlie taught me reliability and dependability.

Chapter Two

Vision

Seeing your life more clearly

'I can see clearly now the rain is gone
I can see all obstacles in my way
Gone are the dark clouds that made me blind
It's gonna be a bright, bright sun shiny day
Look all around, there's nothing but blue skies
Look straight ahead, there's nothing but blues skies.'

Johnny Nash

'Some see things as they are and ask why? I dream of things that never were and ask why not?'

George Bernard Shaw

STORY:

Many years ago I spent a summer as a counsellor on a boys summer camp in a place called Bemidji, Minnesota in the USA (right in the centre of the North American continent). I met many interesting people at the camp and, on reflection, a lot of the experiences I had shaped my later life. But one encounter fits in with the whole issue of vision.

Steve Kenning

Only in recent years have I really understood the need and the power of having a clear vision, but even so, my mind has often gone back to a particular encounter late one night at Camp Thunderbird.

It was about 10 p.m and I was doing my weekly duty at the camp, making sure the boys were all asleep and everything was OK. This was often a pretty pleasant experience as the boys were all very well behaved rich kids, the camp was 15 miles from anywhere and the cabins in which the boys lived were spaced out across a forest on the edge of Lake Plantaganet. Another student, who had just arrived at the camp, was also on duty. This guy was quite weird on first impression, he looked like a surfer and talked as if he was permanently stoned. Talk in the Camp was that he was related to the Kennedys, I think his name was Walker (We all had nicknames, mine was Stretch!). Anyway Walker and I strolled around the camp talking for 10 minutes or so. It was a beautiful still evening and the stars glistened above. Walker told me to stand still and open my eyes and look at everything around me. We stood in silence for a while doing this. Although it was dark, soon you could see a great deal. Walker told me to calmly wait and look at the same spot for a long period of time. I did this and I was amazed by what I saw, things that normally I would have hurriedly missed. Walker then told me to close my eyes and listen. Again after a while I heard sounds I had never ever noticed. Finally, he said look at the stars and look

Positivity

for your self. He said look into the stars and look for your dreams. I did this and it was enormously uplifting. I didn't see my future but through staring into the vast emptiness of space I had all kinds of positive thoughts and visions about my life.

What Walker taught me that night was that you need to stop and look and listen in order to know where you are going. Too often we are too busy and we miss all kinds of opportunities and most important of all we never get to fully understand ourselves.

**'Well most of all nothing much ever really happens,
and God rides high up in the ordinary sky,
until we find ourselves at our most distracted,
and the miracle that was promised,
creeps quietly by'**

Nick Cave

Stimulus

Take any successful journey and it can be broken down to three essential components:

- where you are at any given moment,
- awareness of your surroundings,
- and the destination.

These translate to – current reality, constant feedback and vision.

If you want a journey to be successful, you need to pay close attention to these three factors.

Every journey needs an intended destination, a vision. You might not get to your destination, as the scenery on the journey might get very interesting and lead to a change in the vision, but you need something to aim for. Vision is essential.

Where does the vision come from? This is a really good question, as is: Whose vision is it? There is a tendency to take the setting of a vision lightly, almost creating a vision for the sake of it. Some organisations have such a weak vision that it gets lost and results in a lot of individuals wandering around on unrelated journeys. This kind of situation is common and such organisations don't move forward.

Advice

A vision is likely to develop from a germ of an idea or belief. Conversations, discussions, research, conferences, visits and other influences, help shape the vision. An individual or an organisation needs to really believe in its vision. The vision must be constantly developing. As people travel the journey they take in the current reality and adjust their

Positivity

behaviour accordingly. This inevitably leads to new destinations.

Action Point:

- *Set a destination for yourself for 6 months from now.*
- *Assess where you are at the moment.*
- *What are the strengths/weaknesses of your present situation?*
- *What do you need to do to move from where you are now in order to reach your destination?*

Inspiration:

- Kylie Minogue
    - Apart from being so small and gorgeous, Kylie is inspirational in that she seems to have a very real ability to keep changing her vision successfully! She has also shown real determination in the face of adversity – carrying on with her demanding public life although everyone would have understood if she'd stopped.

Chapter Three

Leadership

Leading yourself towards the best in life

'Every great man is always being helped by everybody, for his gift is to get good out of all things and all persons.'
John Ruskin

Everyone is a leader. The way in which you lead yourself is essential. If you cannot lead your self how can you possibly be expected to lead other people?

STORY:

I have worked for surprisingly few good leaders. Most people in leadership positions are there for reasons of ego and power and care little for others. These people are misguided, as great leaders, who care about and nurture other people, stand head and shoulders above the many pretenders.

The great Joe Wheeler was Headteacher for my first year as Deputy Headteacher at Ercall Wood School in Telford. Joe had been Head for many years and was a year off retirement. Joe was a great leader. He didn't actually appear to do a great deal

Positivity

but he gave people the confidence to do things, to take risks and to work for him. You always wanted to please him and you would be distraught if you let him down. His talent was in the way he treated other people. He was very honest and supported you fully in public, but could be hard on you in private. He regularly boosted your self-esteem with third person affirmations (praising you in front of someone else – very powerful) and he lived what he preached. His style was small conversations in the corridor, but always very timely. He knew what was going on and he regularly stroked the people who were orchestrating the success of his school. One key thing he said to me was: 'Treat everyone as you would wish to be treated yourself'. This statement has always lived with me and I believe it is the key to leadership.

Stimulus

The characteristics of good leaders, these can be applied to leadership in a team, an organisation or simply when leading yourself:

- ❖ Good leaders don't focus on the negative, they focus on the positive.
  People want to feel good about themselves and they look to leaders for this. If you focus on the negative, for example: 'watching out for the rock in the road when you're driving you will probably hit it, whereas if you said 'steer to the left', you would miss the rock'.

People need to feel part of a positive environment if they are to be encouraged and have the confidence to grow.

- ❖ Good leaders make things happen, and in particular they make things happen for individuals.
  This not only makes people feel good and supportive of the leader, it also creates a feeling of momentum, and emotion is generated - the more emotion the faster the change.

- ❖ All really good leaders have an ability to make people feel good when in their presence. This isn't to say that leaders shouldn't have a hard side, because when people do things wrong they need to be put right. As part of leadership training we should reflect on the kind of things good leaders do which don't threaten people – things such as the way they interact with people, their use of humour, and their ability to have status but not to promote it.

- ❖ Good leaders also model being the lead learner and encourage intellectual growth. Through this they build the capacity of others – they develop people as leaders, they extend individuals and they encourage everyone to look outside their comfort zone. Good leaders invest heavily in continuous personal development, set challenging

Positivity

targets and reward people who respond to the challenge.

- ❖ Good leaders also create a strong common ethos amongst the people they work with. This is often achieved by developing a set of shared values and beliefs.

- ❖ Good leaders have vision and constantly measure the current reality in relation to the vision through providing and receiving feedback – they are rarely concerned with where they have come from.

- ❖ Good leaders take control of their future. Through doing this leaders can make the future happen. They don't wait for opportunities to happen, they are ready for it and get themselves and others on the move.

- ❖ Good leaders realise they are on a journey and don't get bogged down with too much strategic long-term planning.

- ❖ Good leaders juggle initiatives
They avoid overload and fragmentation by keeping initiatives as part of the wider vision.

- ❖ Lead learners float ideas and get people thinking

Someone else will then make connections to help move things forward.

Advice:

We can all be good leaders. Leadership is not about leading other people. If you know yourself and are confident about who you are and if you like yourself, then you naturally exude confidence and warmth. People respond to this. People will want to be with you, work with you, listen to you if they trust and believe in you. The answer to becoming a good leader is to learn to lead yourself. Look at your strengths – how can you make the most of them? Focus on your weaknesses – what can you do to improve them or to minimise their impact? What do you need to do to make yourself feel good?

Action Point:

Take a look at your own life and assess your performance against each of the characteristics of good leaders:
- Do you focus more on being positive in your life or are you really generally negative? What good does it do to be negative?
- Do you make things happen? For yourself? For others? Or do you simply find excuses for not doing something?

Positivity

- Do you make other people feel good about themselves? Or are you always trying to get the better of other people?
- Do you have a frame of mind where you continually believe that you are learning? Or do you think you know it all? Just take a moment to think about all the things you have learnt today.
- Do you share your beliefs and values with others? If they are so important to you, which they should be, why not share them?
- Do you have a vision? Are you constantly checking your progress towards your vision? Or do you live in the past?
- Do you take control of your own future? Or are you reliant on other people?
- Do you realise you are on a journey? Are you marooned or are you moving forward?
- Do you juggle lots of different things in your life?
- Do you encourage ideas and try out new things?

Inspiration:

- Tony Blair.
  Listen to him speak, observe the way he deals with people. Whether you like his politics or not, he displays the features of a very good, modern leader.

Steve Kenning

- Joe Strummer (now deceased, sadly, former leader of the punk/rock group 'The Clash' and later a well respected musician in his own right)
  The strength of Joe's beliefs and values were transmitted to me through his music and shaped a lot of my post-adolescent thinking.

Chapter Four

Self-Confidence

I feeeeeeeeeel good!

**'I feel good, I knew that I would,
I feel good, I knew that I would,
So good,
So good.'**

James Brown

'Every man who accomplishes things sees first in his mind what he wishes to do. He puts away all doubt. It makes no difference how small or how large the thing you want to do may be; if you have an unlimited confidence in your ability to do it, you will do it.'

Charles Fillmore

Over recent years I have become increasingly convinced that the process of individual growth is vital for everyone, as it not only helps people to understand themselves, but it helps develop the skills to live and work in the world today. People need not only to understand themselves, but also be able to work well with others, and, most importantly for leaders, to ultimately support the growth of others by being generative. This kind of activity develops self-confidence in everyone, and as Sven Goran Ericksson believes: 'no self-confidence – no success'.

Story:

The Chelsea football club manager in 2005 was Jose Mourinho. The self-confidence Jose exudes is quite phenomenal and is translated into the way his team plays. His self-confidence isn't just manufactured, it is hard earned and is a result of many experiences. Mourinho recognises the moment when he realised he had the self-confidence to be a successful coach. It was during his role as the coach to FC Porto some years before, when they beat Panathinaikos away in the quarter-finals of the UEFA Cup.

'We had lost at home and no Portuguese team had ever earned a point in Greece. We won 2-0 and in that moment I felt I had gone from domestic level to the European standard........Along the way I have been influenced by some people. Even when I was scouting for Bobby Robson around the world I got ideas. ......During my last year at Barcelona (under Louis Van Gaal) I was given the responsibility of taking the team in some friendlies or cup games. Louis would monitor the way I handled things....I had developed my knowledge and confidence. Confidence yes, arrogant no. I

Positivity

am open to people and my friends laugh when they read articles that label me as arrogant. They know it is not true.'

Mourinho.

Self-confidence is borne out of positive experiences and successes. Although success has to be on your own terms. As I developed through various roles of responsibility in schools I always felt unsure before taking on the job, worried that it might be a step too far. Each time I pushed myself out of my comfort zone into a new role, I soon realised that I could handle it and my self-confidence soon grew to such a level that it wasn't long before I was looking for the next job. Even when I became a Headteacher it took me several years to escape the feeling that I was an imposter, about to be found out. After a while though, as you are successful, you relax and your thinking moves on again.

Stimulus

Self-confidence is a strange thing. What creates it is different in every person. There is no doubt that as you get older and as you learn to understand yourself more then you gain in self-confidence. I do wish that I had my present level of self-confidence in my twenties when I was considering my chances with a number of women!

Self-confidence depends on whether:

- o ***We feel*** accepted as a person
- o ***We have*** had basic human love (from our parents?)
- o ***We have*** the confidence to take on responsibility
- o ***We have*** felt free within strict limits
- o ***We have*** felt that someone believed in our talent and prospects.

Advice:

The development of self-confidence, for self and others, is an important part of raising aspirations. If you believe in yourself and feel good about yourself then you are more likely to want to raise your aspirations.

There are a number of key skills and tools that help support individual growth:
- o Self-belief
- o Resilience
- o Self-understanding
- o Self-analysis
- o Self-development
- o Efficacy (ability to make things happen)
- o Humility
- o Ability to manage comfort zones
- o Self-talk
- o Visualisation

The key to all this is to develop a mentality of I WANT TO as opposed to I HAVE TO. If you want

Positivity

to do something you are more likely to develop the motivation to do it, and will then undoubtedly enjoy it.

Action Point:

Over the next few days whatever happens, try to remember that you are totally unique. Nobody else is like you. No one else can make the contribution to the world that you make.

Whatever you do, see the positives. Congratulate yourself when you do something that is good or that works. *Re-live* the positive images in your mind. You want to get those positives to live in your sub-conscious. Even when you make mistakes, look for the positives in what you did and find positive solutions to make sure you don't do the same thing again.

Inspiration:

- **Aki Riihilahti** – The Finnish international footballer, also of Crystal Palace fame, for his attitude to life: **'You can only fail if you stop trying.....I know for sure I will never stop setting goals and having dreams. I want to base my everyday life on it.'**

Steve Kenning

He also said: '**The world is full of unused potential and I would rather crash and burn in trying to live my dreams than not to dare go after them at all.**'

Chapter Five

VISUALISATION

Making what you want a reality

'If your brain can envisage that you can do something, you can do it.'

Arnold Schwarzenegger

When you really want to do something if you then visualise your self doing it time and time again it will become reality in your subconscious and enable it to become *reality*.

Story:

I once heard an excellent visualisation story from someone called Ian Gilbert. I listened carefully and managed to apply it to my own life.

Whenever I go into Plymouth, my local city, I always park in the Mayflower Street car park that is fairly small and tucked away behind some of the shops. I like parking there as it's very handy for the main shopping area. Ian Gilbert taught me to visualise what you want. So, in the case of a car parking space, I simply visualise a space appearing in what is a very busy car park. Every time I go shopping in Plymouth I spend the 20 minute car journey visualising a parking space. Believe it or not, it works. I might have to drive round the car park several times but there is nearly always a space for me!

Stimulus

Everyone sees things differently. This is particularly the case when looking at things inside your head. I'm the kind of person who sees things in pictures. It is very easy for me to visualise things because of this. I love reading very descriptive books that conjure up an atmosphere as my imagination turns the story into a moving picture in my mind.

However you may see things in your mind, we all visualise things. Many of us visualise things all the time without really realising it. We run things that have happened to us through our minds, often again and again, sometimes adding improvements or accentuating our view of things.

When we really want something or are worried about something it is very hard to get the particular image out of your mind. Love is a classic example. When you fall in love all your visual images of the person you love are amazing, you don't notice or

Positivity

think of anything bad about them as your brain is trying to convince your sub-conscious that this person is the right one for you. You blot out the fact that the beautiful blonde you have just fallen in love with might be revealing slight evidence of some darker roots!

Our brain is immensely powerful. If we can convince ourselves that we can do something then we can do it. Look at any sprinter or high jumper just before their race or jump and you will see them visually preparing themselves for success.

I always treat visualisation as a form of cost/benefit analysis. I do it like this:

- I think about what I want to achieve. I set the vision of success first. What are the potential benefits?
- I then visualise the path to success. What stages do I go through to get there? What do I have to do?
- The next stage is looking at the potential problems. How can I overcome each of these eventualities and at what cost?
- Finally, having considered all possible benefits and costs, actions and reactions, I visualise the whole process from starting point to success, over and over again until I believe what I am visualising. It does work. When it doesn't it is normally either something that is very much out of my hands, such as

winning the lottery, or when someone wants something more than I do and their visualisation is more powerful.

Advice

Visualise what you want and believe that you can achieve it. Plan in your mind the worst-case scenario. See yourself being successful but work out responses to the possible pitfalls. Make sure that your dream is strong enough, don't be weak, believe you can overcome anything.

Action Point:

Think of something you need to do but are not particularly keen to do. It could be something like: speaking in front of a group of people, dealing with a difficult colleague/customer, driving somewhere new and confusing, performing, etc. Now imagine yourself doing the task in your head. Run through the task from start to finish in the exact way in which you hope it will go. Do this *<u>visualisation</u>* exercise as many as a hundred times in your head. Eventually it will be part of your current reality and it will be etched strongly onto your sub-consciousness and the chances of the task going well will be massively enhanced. ***Try it!***

Positivity

Inspiration:

- David **Beckham** – he has done it several times, although the equalising goal he scored, some years ago, from a free kick in the World Cup qualifier against Greece was one of the best examples of visualisation you will ever see. If you get the chance to see it again look at his face, you can see that he can visualise scoring.

Chapter Six

Open Your Mind

Looking at things through a different set of eyes

> *'Don't be afraid to give your best to what seemingly are small jobs. Every time you conquer one it makes you that much stronger. If you do the little jobs well, the big ones will tend to take care of themselves.'*
>
> *Dale Carnegie*

Routine becomes part of all of our lives. It would be very difficult to live without some kind of routine. Routine varies – some people do the same thing everyday, such as catch a train at the same time, get out of bed, and so on. Some people have weekly routines – doing the shopping on the same day, playing football, going to a dance class, going to the pub. Other routines are more spaced out – visiting parents or friends, birthdays, etc. We need some routine, in fact routine can be quite satisfying and comforting – you are confident, aware and generally safe in a situation you are familiar with.

Linked to routine though is complacency, familiarity and dependency. Dangerous words!

Positivity

We all need stimulus, challenge and excitement. We need, at times, to get the adrenalin flowing. This does not often happen during routine operations. If it does it is unexpected and as a result can be quite stressful. What we all need to do is to look for the unexpected!

Story:

I am a great believer in the benefits of new experiences and in grasping any opportunity to break from the routine. A few weeks ago my wife and I just decided we needed such a break from our routine. Like many people we work very hard, we give most of our free time to looking after the needs of our children and it was late November, full of rain and dark nights. We thought briefly about the impending build up to Christmas – the need to buy presents, get a tree and put up decorations, as well as the build up to the end of the year at work – yet we decided to break free from the routine.

I mentioned earlier that we are big fans of a singer called Nick Cave. We had spotted a few weeks earlier that Nick Cave and the Bad Seeds were on a European tour. At the time we couldn't make any of the British dates, due to other commitments. In fact the only date we could possibly make was a Saturday night, late November in Lausanne, Switzerland. As we didn't even know where Lausanne was and it was abroad this was immediately discounted. Anyway, that week I happened to be in London and saw a poster for really cheap flights to Geneva. Later that day when I was driving home I was listening to Nick Cave. For some reason I wondered if Lausanne was near to Geneva, so I looked on the internet and it was. So there and then we decided to go to Lausanne to see Nick Cave and the Bad Seeds. How exciting. I'd never done something quite so impulsive as this.

We thought for a while about the possible problems of such a jaunt:
- Cost
- how tired we would be
- waiting around at airports
- the travel involved
- our ignorance about Lausanne and how to get there
- was Nick Cave worth it?
- where would we stay?
- what if Swiss rock concerts are violent affairs?
- and every other reason for not going.

Perhaps the greatest problem was that every Saturday I coached my son's football team and I would have to miss a game – something I had never done. As we talked though, we got more and more excited about the possibility of a weekend away.

More effort was required though:

Positivity

- I searched the internet for the Lausanne Metropole where the concert was to be staged and eventually found that tickets were to be handled by a German company.
- I phoned the company and asked if they had tickets for the concert in Lausanne. A German comedian stated that they had no tickets for a concert in Lausanne. I was a bit dismayed, as I thought our exciting weekend was now not going to happen. When he replied I realised that he was having a little joke with my pronunciation, he added with a chuckle: 'we have no tickets for a concert in LORsanne, but we do have for LOWsanne.' I applauded him for his wicked humour and then booked the tickets.
- The next stage was booking the flights. We couldn't go from Bristol, but we got tickets from Luton – late Friday evening outbound, returning Sunday morning.
- Next was somewhere to stay. Onto the internet again, and we found and booked a cheapish hotel not far from the concert hall.

The weekend came and we had a tremendous time. A meal in a real characterful Swiss style restaurant on Friday evening enjoying people watching, a few beers in a disco/bar assessing the night-life of Lausanne, a walk in the sun by the side of Lake Geneva on Saturday followed by pleasant afternoon window shopping and drinking coffee, beer, etc. Then a gentle stroll up to the Metropole Concert Hall. This building was superbly reconditioned and revealed all its art-deco styling. Our tickets were for standing in the lower concert hall – what a show!

We arrived home in Devon mid Sunday afternoon. We are still, months later, living on what was almost a life-changing weekend. We had chance and time to talk about some very important issues, we had a wonderfully relaxing time and we haven't stopped listening to Nick Cave since. So, the weekend was worth it but the point of the story is that if you break out of your usual routine, open your eyes and look at things you would not normally see, you learn and you develop.

So what did we learn from our Lausanne experience?
- Swiss women seem to get more attractive as they get older.
- Lausanne is a pleasant provincial town, and very wealthy.
- Horse meat is a good substitute for beef
- Swiss wine is good.
- Swiss trains are double-deckers and fantastic.
- Always buy a single train ticket if you are travelling in Switzerland for more than a day.
- Geneva Airport is much better organised than Luton Airport.
- Nick Cave is a god!

Positivity

Stimulus

Our brains are very complex and respond to all kind of different stimuli. I have always felt it is better to try to exercise your brain yourself rather than let it be exercised by others.

What I mean by this, is that if you are in control and are looking for challenge and stimulus, then your brain will always be on the alert. Then you can manage almost any scenario as your brain is fit, healthy and alert. If, on the other hand, you let things happen to you because you are scared or too lazy to break from your routine then you may find life and any unexpected new experiences difficult to cope with and possibly quite stress inducing.

Our brains enjoy learning. One type of brain operation is known as the Reticular Activating System (RAS) and this makes us aware of things that are important to us. Imagine then in your daily routine, your RAS is mainly just bringing to your attention the same old things. BUT you decide it's time to buy a new car, possibly a BMW 5 series (we can all dream!). All you see then on your travels are BMW 5 series cars, yet you didn't notice them before. Your RAS is helping you to justify and convince your sub-conscious that you are a pretty smart cookie to want such an affordable and much sought after car, after all lots of other people have made the same decision. This feeling is pretty good. When your RAS picks up something new on your radar it is quite exciting and energising.

Advice

If you look for new opportunities and new experiences on a more regular basis your RAS will tune in and help you feel more energised, more excited and generally more alive. Try it, it is true!

Action Point:

This week do five things that are different to the things you normally do. One of these things should be something you have never done before. It could be something major or something small, like using an electric toothbrush for the first time. Do it!

At the end of the week, evaluate. It will almost certainly have been a more invigorating week than the norm.

Inspiration:

- The intrepid pioneers who settled the new world in the past centuries. Particularly those who went to America. I dislike the way in which the complete North American Indian civilisation was destroyed by these pioneers, although you have to admire the courage and sheer drive of these people. Often they were heading into the complete unknown. Their RAS's must have been working overtime!

Chapter Seven

Learn Something New

What did you learn today?

'The only dumb question is the question you don't ask.'

Anon.

I'm forty-nine years old but I live in a perpetual stage of expectation and excitement. My mind is stuck at that fascinating pre-pubescent time where life is an adventure and everything is interesting. The time before you hit the teenage years of knowing everything and nothing.

With the mind of a 12 year old in the ageing body of a 49 year old, life can be interesting, as your body will not always do what your mind thinks it can – snowboarding brings painful memories!

What makes me see everything as a new experience? Why do I want to try out new things? Why am I such a risk taker? I really don't know the answers to these questions.

Some of it is undoubtedly in the genes, some is down to your conditioning and the role models and experiences you have had throughout your life. I do believe though that anyone can develop a positive, inquiring mind if they want to. An essential stage to achieving this is developing a desire to learn new things. We learn new things all the time, but when you actively decide to learn something new it is far more rewarding and can lead to other exciting opportunities.

'I tell you one thing. I've been to a parallel universe, I've seen time running backwards, I've played pool with planets, and I've given birth to twins, but I never thought in my entire life I'd taste an edible Pot Noodle.'

Craig Charles as Lister in Red Dwarf.

Story:

I can't remember learning a great deal at school, apart from how many cows there are in Argentina, a fact that has been eternally useful to me throughout my life, as you can no doubt imagine! Socially, though, school was excellent and it was brilliant for sport. What school did teach me were the skills of social interaction, for which I am eternally grateful. Also, all the knowledge and activities I experienced at school together have given me a solid foundation of general skills and knowledge.

I learn all the time. Today, for example, I have learnt many things, here are a few of them:
- Siddhartha was The Buddha.

Positivity

- How to put a weekly appointment into the organiser function of my mobile phone.
- General Franco was a very small man.
- The Tsunami that destroyed much of the low lying land around the Indian Ocean in late 2004 actually reached as far as the African coast.
- It snowed in the French Alps last week.
- You can severely damage your back without knowing it.
- Lights are used to dry plaster.

The major things I have learnt in my life so far have taken different forms:

- I am still learning about myself, although when I was about 44 years old I really started to know myself for the first time. This has taken a lot of thought, self-analysis and learning. This has been a very worthwhile process, as today I have never been happier.
- When I started teaching Geography, everything I had learned at school and University proved to be quite useless. I had to re-learn everything in order to learn how to teach it. For the first time though, there was quite a lot of it I actually understood through teaching it.
- I took up the guitar when I was 14 years old but learnt to play the bass guitar when I was 38 years old. This has paid off and I have played bass guitar in a seven-piece rock

band for most of the past ten years. I still find it hard to believe that people actually paid us to perform at weddings, parties, etc!
- I started skiing last year. This has taken real determination, especially as it takes me much longer to pick up the basics than anyone else in the family. However, I'm progressing well now and I love it!
- I really have great problems learning languages, but my next target is to learn Spanish. Who knows maybe I will then get to spend much more time in the lovely city of Barcelona!

My aim is to keep learning and to keep an active interest in people and everything around me. I am convinced that you live much longer if you are a lifelong learner.

Stimulus:

Learning cannot be satisfactorily achieved in isolation. We often learn best with and through other people. What we all need to do is to develop a positive attitude to our learning and in so doing, create a climate for learning.

An easy thing to do is to talk about your learning, share your learning and to help other people to learn. Learning provides opportunities to develop. All learning is good as it all helps you to move forward as a person. Learning is particularly

Positivity

important as it raises your self-confidence and your self-knowledge. The key to a positive and happy life is to achieve a fairly high level of personal mastery.

Advice

The eight conditions for raising aspirations, mentioned earlier, provide a good framework for learning. Think deeply about how you can apply them to your life.

Action Point:

On any one-day, make a note of everything that you learn: new knowledge, new ways of doing things, etc. You will be surprised by how much learning you do.

Every month choose a learning target. Make it realistic but enjoyable: ride a bike, use a glue gun, paint a picture, learn a language, wind-surf, knit. Whatever you decide to learn, you will grow as a person. Even if you give up after a few minutes you will have learnt something and learnt a lot about yourself.

Inspiration:

- Anyone you see on the nursery slopes of a ski centre. It takes a lot of learning of all sorts to learn to ski, to be in *control* and not to emit strange cries of **fear**.

Chapter Eight

Opportunity

Life is full of surprises – be on the look out for them

'We all have big changes in our lives that are more or less a second chance.'

Harrison Ford

My first awareness of what is a very 'round' word 'opportunities', was when The Clash pumped out a jovial little number called 'Career Opportunities' in the late 1970's:

'Career opportunities, the ones that never knock, every job they offer you is to keep you out the dock.'

Joe Strummer and the rest of The Clash really shaped my thinking in the late seventies/early eighties, in particular I started thinking about the opportunities in life and the need to grasp them.

Opportunities happen to us all, sometimes quite unexpectedly. Many opportunities presented to us are not taken up. Why? Maybe we are scared of breaking out of our comfort zones, or perhaps we

Positivity

don't recognise opportunities. For whatever reason, missed opportunities are something to be regretted - who knows where an opportunity taken could lead you?

Story:

A really good colleague of mine in a previous school was a wonderful lady called, Anita Burgoyne. Anita had been at the school for thousands of years and had fulfilled many senior roles. Anita found my approach and insensitivities quite hard to stomach early on but eventually we developed a very professional and strong relationship. She put me right in many situations and helped me to develop!

After a couple of years of working with her, Anita, who was a diligent hard worker, started to develop a lot of illnesses and was finding the pressures of her job quite draining. Anita went on a course centred on basic psychology and designed to help people make the most of their lives. Anita came back from this course invigorated. She had taken on board the principles and was beginning to live them, the course tutor had also recognised her as a possible real talent for facilitating these courses. Anita was then trained up as a facilitator.

Later in the year Anita decided to take early retirement. Something she had wanted to do for a number of years but had felt she couldn't afford to.

Through a number of things – ill health and the programme she had been on in particular – she realised that there were many things she wanted to do in her life, all she had to do was to take the opportunities open to her.

Anita is now retired. She still earns some money by facilitating courses based at her old school, a little supply teaching, visiting theatres around the world, and enjoying the delights of her garden whenever she wishes! I saw Anita recently and she looked fantastic and her ailments have all gone. All this has happened due to Anita grasping and creating a range of opportunities in the later years of her teaching career. This is quite amazing if you consider that for many years she took advantage of very few opportunities. The change that enabled her to make the most of the opportunities presented to her was the encouragement others gave her to get her to think about what she really wanted in life and to make things happen for herself. This she did with great results!

Stimulus:

If someone offered you three years in *Barcelona*, in a nice sea front three bed apartment and a decent tax-free salary for doing very little. Would you:

- **Accept the offer without reservation?**
- **Consider the offer for a few days?**
- **Refuse the offer?**

Positivity

Your response to this very much depends on your current situation and your responsibilities. If you are fairly newly married with a couple of young children you may consider it a risk not worth taking. However if you are later or earlier in life with fewer responsibilities it may be the move for you.

A guy into whose job I succeeded, once gave me some pretty poor advice. He said **'never volunteer, but never turn down an opportunity'**. This is poor advice in that sometimes if you don't make it obvious that you are keen to take on new things the opportunities don't arise.

I now spend much of my time creating opportunities for staff and students. If one opportunity engages one person then it could change a life. Few people know their true path in life. It is only by experiencing things you don't expect that someone can truly find their real life.

Each of us can get stuck into a life that is adequate, it is only by experimenting with life that we find true fulfilment. Are you truly fulfilled? If not, which is realistically what you are thinking right now, how can you create the opportunities to make more of your life?

Advice

If you close your mind and exist in a finely tuned routine then very few opportunities are going to arise in your life. To open your life to opportunities you need to have:

- *Aspirations or ambitions.*
- *A desire to learn and develop.*
- *Be prepared to take some risks.*
- *An open mind.*

Opportunities are out there. You have to want to experience them. If you do then you will grow and develop as a person. This is a scary thought as you may consider your present life to be unsatisfactory. *Are you prepared to take the opportunity this book is providing you to take the risk?*

Action Point

The next opportunity that is presented to you, whatever it is – to go to Gateshead on a business trip, to go on a blind date with your friend's sister, to bet on a dead-cert horse – take it. Not every opportunity taken produces the results you want, but you need to get used to making the most of opportunities because you learn from every one, and some bring you pleasures you could never envisage.

Positivity

Inspiration:

- **Harrison Ford** – he was an unknown actor who got his chance in Star Wars. An opportunity he took and as Hans Solo he was *so good* it set up his future career in films.

Chapter Nine

Fun and Excitement

Have a good laugh

'People who laugh actually live longer than those who don't laugh. Few persons realize that health actually varies according to the amount of laughter.'

James J. Walsh

I have never been able to understand miserable people. True, I'm miserable sometimes, but not for long and normally my miserableness is tinged with some humour. This is a real weakness of mine – this lack of affinity with moaners. Life is too short, every minute of everyday is sacred, that's why I hate queuing and other time wasting activities. Why be miserable? There are real pressures, stresses and sadnesses that we all face and they do make you unhappy for a time. The miserableness I'm referring to is when people are miserable for most of the time despite basically having a good life.

I've known people be miserable because they have to do the washing. The answer is don't do the washing but put up with wearing smelly clothes!

Positivity

I've known people be miserable because they've got to go to work. The answer is don't go, get a new job or go without the money!

I've known people be miserable because they think they are too fat. The answer, take things into your own hands and lose weight.

I've known people be miserable because their football team lost. The answer is get a life!

People are nearly always miserable because they feel they are being done to, in other words they are not in control of their own lives. Often their miserableness becomes so embedded in their psyche that they can't see any way out of their situation.

Taking some self-responsibility to make things happen for yourself and laughter are two ways of reducing miserableness.

Laughter in particular makes you and other people feel good. People respond to people who are good-natured. Friendships are easier to make, managing and leading people is made much, much easier and you will probably live a lot longer if you bring humour into your life.

Story:

Like most fathers I think my children are great. My daughter, who is 14 years old, is a real comedienne.

Steve Kenning

She doesn't tell jokes but she is always, well mostly – apart from the growing teenage tantrums – in a good mood. Her funniest feature is her habit of making up or extending words as part of her normal conversation. Things like: 'I'm going on the tramopoline' (Trampoline), 'trousees' (trousers), 'exhaustipated' (exhausted), 'shoesees' (shoes), she also can't say ventriloquist, but then who can? So whenever she is around there is a lovely atmosphere.

Today though I had some fun and excitement. The weather was atrocious, really wet and very windy. It had been raining all day and there were puddles everywhere and the ground was waterlogged. As you can imagine, as it was a Sunday, the vast majority of people were having a very relaxing time in their warm, dry houses. Me included. However, my wife, Paula, and I have set ourselves a target of going for a three mile run three times a week. Having got out of bed and dressed in our running gear we looked outside and decided to wait until the nasty rain went away. At three o'clock though it was worse than ever. As our favoured run is out of town, down some country lanes and across a park we had to go before dark. I bullied Paula, in the nicest possible way, into going for the run. She was not happy. By the end of the first mile we were totally soaked and wind battered. We were running through puddles with no care, despite soggy shoes, and started to sing 'singin' in the rain' and dancing in the puddles. This led to a good conversation, well, as good a conversation you can have when

Positivity

you are very unfit and are two miles into your run, beginning the uphill section. We were laughing about the fact that we had pushed ourselves out of our comfort zones into some very bad weather. We were having a really good laugh in the rain, whereas we would otherwise be in the house reading, working or watching TV. The point of this story is that even in the most ordinary of situations and circumstances, you can have fun.

Stimulus:

A great story on the impact of humour and good-naturedness is to be found at the start of Daniel Goleman's book *'Emotional Intelligence'*. I won't repeat the whole story here but it is basically about a New York bus driver who greets every new passenger with delight and good humour. This type of behaviour is infectious and raises the spirits of all the passengers regardless of their mood.

A good friend of mine, Paul Bordeaux, an educational consultant and a great thinker on human psychology, relates this kind of behaviour to what he calls emotional IOU's. If you are pleasant to people and make them laugh, then they go to the next person in a good mood and make them feel good, and so on. The reverse is also very true. Imagine that the Managing Director at your place of work has had a terrible day. He or she might tear a strip off one of his managers, making him or her feel really low. They are likely to come across you in a very bad mood and give you a hard time, possibly for no real reason. You then go home and take it out on the wife, the kids or a packet of biscuits! This transference of mood can be extremely negative and unproductive in a business sense but also in personal circumstances. How many arguments start because one of you is in a bad mood and are totally unreasonable with the other person?

On the other hand by bringing fun and excitement into peoples lives you can have a very positive effect. Fun and excitement isn't always about jokes and laughter. It can be any situation where you are being challenged, in a good way. If you can get yourself, or others, to think, then you are setting a challenge. This is invariably exciting and is often fun.

Advice

Take responsibility to improve your own life. When you feel miserable analyse the reasons. If it is someone else's fault analyse further. Are you sure it is their fault or do you share some of the blame? Whatever, take responsibility and make sure, that before you interact with anyone, you are in a more positive mood.

Try very hard to control your outward vibes. What messages are you giving off to other people? Observe how people behave towards you

Positivity

depending on the mood you are emanating. If you can give off positive vibes you will make people want to know you, perhaps even want to love you, want to work for you and want to be in your company. You will also feel much better about yourself.

I know that I give off an almost permanent good vibe. When I look anything other than happy people ask me if I am all right. But this positive, good-humouredness is a very infectious trait and it now permeates my organisation.

Action Point

Today, for at least the whole day, make sure that you are bright, sunny and funny with everyone. You haven't got to tell jokes, just smile, compliment people and be generally good-natured. Avoid letting anyone wind you up or get you annoyed, just smile at them and move on. At the end of the day assess how successful you were. *How do you feel? How productive was the day?*

Inspiration:

There are endless names here, mostly from my youth, but you may have heard of them:

- **Stuart Hall** – his commentary on *'It's a Knockout'* (International Edition) was hilarious.

Steve Kenning

- **John Noakes** – a Blue Peter presenter in the 1970's. Everything was possible and everything was fun with John.
- **Indiana Jones, Han Solo** (Star Wars) – all action, and good fun.
- **Kris Akabusi** – the 1980's athlete. He was always laughing!
- **Gwen Stefani** – well, she looks all fun and excitement to me!

Chapter Ten

Time

Are you a time lord or a time slave?

'Striving for excellence motivates you; striving for perfection is demoralizing.'

Harriet Braiker

Time is something that fascinates us all. We are pre-occupied with its passing and our ageing, we are forever trying to find more time and are very adept at wasting it for other people! If we could manage time effectively we would be happier. This is probably very true. Some people seem to glide serenely through life with the time to do all the things they want to do, when they want to do them.

When you play football at an increasingly higher level, you notice that the players you are now playing with are not necessarily any more skilful than the ones you used to play with, they simply see things more quickly and appear to have more time to do things with the ball. It is the same at work. Some people always seem to be burdened with a massive amount of work, and they are forever telling others about it! Yet there are people who achieve a great deal but don't seem to be under pressure of work. How do they do it?

Steve Kenning

When you have developed the ability to manage and control your use of time you can class yourself as a 'Time Lord'. Alternatively, if you are forever under pressure and complaining about your lack of time to do the things you wish then you are most certainly a 'Time Slave'.

Father Ted TV programme:

<u>Dougal</u>: *'God, I've never seen a clock at 5 a.m before!'*

Story:

Some years ago there was a very popular comedy series called *'The Rise and Fall of Reginald Perrin'* that starred Leonard Rossiter. In the early episodes Reggie Perrin (Leonard Rossiter), was locked into a life of what appeared to be real drudgery. He lived in the suburbs and travelled by train into his job in the city. Everyday he left his house at the same time, kissed his wife goodbye and walked to the train station.

Everyday Reggie arrived at work, hung his hat, coat and umbrella on the coat stand and stated to his secretary, **'Fifteen minutes late, leaves on the line at South Wimbledon,'** or something very similar. He wasn't particularly phased or stressed out by his regular lateness as he was pretty numbed by his whole life. What this did show was that Reggie was not in control of any part of his life, which he hated, least of all his transport to work. Reggie Perrin managed this stress in his life by faking his death and disappeared to another life via the open sea.

Stimulus:

Time management is all about knowing.

Knowing yourself, knowing what is important to you, knowing what you want, knowing how to prioritise and manage your life.

Time management is essential if you want to avoid stress, enjoy life and make the most of your life. Easier said than done? Just think about it. There are 24 hours in the day, and although some people find this not to be enough, this is all there is.

We sleep for about 8 hours of the day and eat for another 1 hour on average. Two hours roughly can be expected to be spent travelling to and from work, with about 8 hours a day probably spent working. Dressing, washing, grooming and other bodily functions take a further hour leaving about 4 hours a day for yourself to do as you please. That is unless you've got children a dog or a very demanding partner! In which case you probably have very little time to yourself.

The key to managing your time in such a busy age is to enjoy everything you do as much as possible. If you hate doing things then it puts pressure on time. Do the things with enjoyment and find ways to spend less time doing them. One key skill you need to learn is to prioritise. This is very hard to master, but if you do the things that are essential or important to you, then some of the other tasks will either become less important or go away. I started using this technique some years ago and it is amazing how many tasks disappear when left for a couple of days.

Advice

Avoid complaining about never having enough time to do things. If you are regularly under pressure to get things done at work then you need to:
- ***Prioritise.*** *Is everything essential?*
- ***Look at your performance.*** *Are you expecting perfection every time? Are you as efficient with your time as you could be? Is there a quicker or better way of working?*
- ***If things don't improve*** *perhaps you seriously need to look at another job or even another career.*

If you are under pressure for time generally, you need to look at what you actually need to do. *Are you in a routine that is difficult to escape? Do the people you live with do their fair share?* Analyse your use of time and take some kind of action.

Positivity

Remember you only live once, so make the most of your life.

Action Point

If today, at any time, you start to feel under pressure of time, just stop what you are doing and take a break, get a coffee. Think about how you could do this job differently. Could you delegate some of the tasks or get someone else to do it? Is there a short cut? Whatever, analyse the task, your performance and the urgency of the task. Go back to the task and, if possible, approach it differently. Even if this doesn't work you will feel better for taking a break.

Inspiration:

- **Doctor Who** – he had the ability, via his Tardis, to go wherever he wanted in time. If he made a mistake he could just go back and put things right.

Chapter Eleven

Values

What's your life worth?

'The true meaning of life is to plant trees, under whose shade you do not expect to sit.'

Nelson Henderson

What are your real values? In other words, what to you is most worthy, what do you prize more than anything else in relation to the way you or others behave? Values come from your emotional self.

It all relates to the value or worth of your life. When you do something or see something that is in direct contradiction to your own values you feel bad, when you do something that supports your values you feel good. Where your values come from depends on the experiences and conditioning you have had throughout your life. People in a particular society do, tend to have a very similar set of values, although they often reveal themselves in different ways and at different levels. This is because the society you are brought up in imposes and conditions you to certain things. A middle-eastern country would probably have very different

Positivity

values to a western European country due to the way of life, religion, culture, etc.

The basic values for people in western cultures, I believe, are mainly centred around respect. Respect for yourself, for others and for living things. If your values involve things such as trust and honesty, these kinds of values are very centred on respect.

How do your values relate to this idea?

How closely do you stick to your values?

Story:

Several years ago I worked with a colleague called Bob Van Demme. Bob was Dutch, brought up mainly in Madrid, where his father was a diplomat, but he had got his teaching qualification in England. Bob was a really nice guy, great fun to be with and had very clear values. His values were very centred around respect. He was immensely honest, dutiful, hardworking, intensely loyal, had a real sense of right and wrong, and was extremely respectful of women. Bob was also very confused, almost certainly as a result of the slight differences in the values systems he had been subject to throughout his life. He would talk about how different life in Holland was to life in Spain was to life in England. The longer he spent in England the more troubled he became. He wrestled with his values constantly.

Bob found the English sense of humour particularly hard to handle. The English do like to run each other and themselves down in often harmless humour. Bob saw this as disrespectful. He also couldn't understand the English sense of fair play. He was 6'5" and had been coached to a high level in Spain at Basketball. We played together in a team called the 49'ers, so called as we spent all our time travelling to games up and down the A49. The league we played in was of a reasonable standard, although Bob really stood out in terms of quality. Bob found it hard to cope with the acceptance of off the ball nudges, knocks, etc which are very much part of the English game. He would get very incensed with the lack of fairness and un-gentlemanly conduct. His value system was being constantly tested.

Over the five or so years he lived over here, he did change. His values became far less idealistic and as a result he became far less happy. In order to fit in with the society he was living in, he had had to surrender some of his values. In the end he decided that he wasn't going to accept this. He got a job In Dubai and met a Canadian woman, who he married in the Rockies, and he now works in Bangkok. We are still occasionally in touch. I don't know, but I assume that in his stateless existence, moving from one culture to another, that he is able to retain his core values and so remain happy.

Positivity

Stimulus:

Father Ted:

'I'm not a fascist. I'm a priest. Fascists dress up in black and tell people what to do. Whereas priests……more drink!'

We all have values, although some of us don't realise that they drive our life and behaviour. The key to living a fruitful and fulfilling life is to become acutely aware of your values, sharpen them up and start living to them. If you do you will undoubtedly feel much better about yourself. This is again another situation where you need to take control of your own life.

Advice

- Take some time to analyse your life:
    - When is it that you get angry or annoyed with other people? Is it when they cross your values?
    - When you are particularly unhappy, is it because you are not behaving in the way that you want to in relation to your values?
- Clarify the values that lie in your sub-conscious. What makes you tick?

- What do you need to do and how do you need to behave to help you live to your values?

The key to a happy and successful life is to never compromise your values, that is if you first of all understand your values!

Action Point

Answer these questions now!

- What is the main thing that gets you up ready for work every morning? The money, loyalty, self-esteem, fear?
- What is the kind of behaviour that really annoys you? Selfishness, dishonesty, loudness, injustice, etc?
- What issues do you continually harp on about to your friends, kids, etc? Work ethic, laziness, honesty, etc?
- What is the underlying factor that makes you unhappy? Self-worth, lack of control, your own mistakes or negative behaviour, the way you treat people, etc?

There are many other questions you could ask yourself all with the aim of identifying your real core values.

Discover your four or five core values and really work at them over a week. At the end of the week

Positivity

assess your success at sticking to them. *How do you feel?*

Inspiration:

- **Sean Connery** – the actor. Sean Connery gives the vibe that everything in life is to be enjoyed. He values life and every aspect of it. Every piece of life forms part of a much bigger jigsaw. Without one part you may not get the other parts, so make the most of it all.
- Anyone who enjoys your company and makes you feel good.

Chapter Twelve

Beliefs

You are what you believe

'There's a man who spoke wonders
Though I've never met him
He said 'He who seeks finds
And who knocks will be let in'.'

Nick Cave

Values and beliefs always confuse me. What is the difference and does it matter? I don't think it does matter at all, as long as you do believe in something and you have standards that you value.

Belief is essential. If you don't believe in anything then what is the point in living? Belief is the engine to your life. It is the very essence of who you are and who you want to be. Values are, on the other hand, things that are important to you in relation to the way you and others should behave.

Some people have such a clear set of beliefs that you can clearly identify them from their actions and from what they say. Other people are either unsure about their beliefs or keep them hidden from others.

Positivity

You are what you believe. Your belief drives you. If this is the case then why hide it? Look at any well-known, successful person. Every one of them has clear beliefs and you can read them. Sir Alex Ferguson, Manager of Manchester United, is driven by his belief in the way football should be played. This goes way beyond football, it relates to human behaviour and psychology. Michael Caine, the actor, is driven by a belief in the way actors should behave and conduct themselves. Tony Blair, has a very clear set of beliefs for the way our society should operate.

Story:

Beliefs are strange things and they do make you behave in certain ways.

An old friend of mine, whom I have unfortunately lost contact with, Christof Bierkopf, a German teacher who lived in the wonderful city of Nuremberg, was great company. He had a great love and knowledge of his home city. His circle of friends and acquaintances was very wide-ranging and he was loved by them all, men and women alike. Despite this, Christof was not married and he couldn't get a relationship to last. Yet he desperately wanted a long and loving relationship with a woman.

Christof's problem was that he believed himself to be too overbearing and smothering with women he liked. This belief was so strong in his mind that it always became reality.

Christof would meet a woman, often through his friends and acquaintances and they would have a wonderful time. Christof would be relaxed and very charming in their company. This made him very attractive to women. However, as soon as any woman showed signs of being relatively interested in him more than just as a social friend, he would become overbearing and very smothering. This always led the women to back off, resisting his approaches, but always wanting to stay in touch with him. This of course made him unhappy and dissatisfied. Christof had many woman friends, all of whom really liked his company, but none of them wanted or could tolerate a more intimate relationship with him.

Christof's belief in the way he was could not be moved. He knew his problem but, almost, as a self-defence against getting too involved with a woman, he would not change his belief.

Stimulus:

The story of Christof is designed to show the power of belief. Christof could change this belief if he really wanted to, but for whatever reason he did not want to. However, the strength of belief made him behave in a certain way.

Father Ted:

Dougal:
'God, I've heard about those cults Ted. People dressing up in black and saying Our Lord's going to come back and save us all.'
Ted:
'No, Dougal, that's us. That's Catholicism.'
Dougal:
'Oh right.'

Understanding your beliefs is important. If you have a strong belief then it can shape your life. A life driven by a strong set of beliefs can be very satisfying as it gives you a strong sense of purpose. Teachers, nurses, doctors, social workers all have a strong belief in helping others. This is a motivator and a source of self-worth for many of them.

Advice

Returning to the question posed at the start of this book, *'What is the meaning of life?'* or perhaps *'What is the purpose of your life?'*

If you have a strong belief then the question is answered. People with a strong sense of purpose or a clear belief know what their life is all about.

If you haven't got a definite belief that drives your life maybe your current life is not for you. Maybe you have a very definite belief in your present life but you just cannot see it. Beliefs do not have to be grand in scale. A belief could be simply that:

- You believe we should do all we can as individuals to protect the environment. If this is your belief then you act in a way that supports your belief – you recycle, you eat organic food, you use renewable energy, etc.
- You believe that a mother should bring up her own children. In this case you would not be a working mother.
- You believe that keeping fit leads to a longer life. If so, then you need to exercise on a regular basis.

When you discover your belief, you have to live it.

Action Point

Are there a couple of things you feel strongly about? If so, hang on to them for a minute, if not, develop a couple of things you feel you could believe in. List the things that are important to you.

Take these beliefs and consider how you need to behave in order to make them real to your life. Live with these actions and beliefs for a while. If you do, and if you put your heart into it, you will find a real purpose in life.

Positivity

Inspiration:

- **Status Quo** – the rock band. I remember seeing them play live at Ingestre Village Hall for 50p in the seventies. This was some years after their hits in the sixties, like *'Pictures of Matchstickmen'*. They had fallen from stardom and were on the road, re-inventing themselves. They believed in their ability and they believed in their music. The worked hard, stuck to it and the rest is history.

Chapter Thirteen

Changing Habits

Life is for living

'Twenty years from now you will be more disappointed by the things you didn't do than by the ones you did do. So throw off the bowlines. Sail away from the safe harbour. Catch the trade winds in your sails. Explore. Dream. Discover.'

Mark Twain

It is sometimes quite astonishing how much our daily life is habitualised. It is even harder to realise and understand how much you depend on your habits. The problem with habits is that they are comfortable. You have to think little when you are following a habit. Have you ever driven on your usual route to work and not remembered passing certain landmarks?

Habits lead to comfort and laziness. It is only when you break out of your habits that you learn new things.

Story

When I was in my thirties I lived in a really pretty market town in the hills of deepest Shropshire. I

Positivity

had a good job, was well involved with the very active community and generally enjoyed life. Everyday I would get up and walk to work. Each Friday after work a number of us would go for several drinks in one of the pubs as it was market day, I would go to the weekly film club showing, go swimming once a week and play for the local football team once a week. I was very good at my job, achieving success and promotions at the same place.

I had been there for seven years when a senior figure from the larger organization, his name was Mike Norton, took me aside one-night at a training evening in a local hotel. He said to me that I had about another year to either decide to stay put and to continue my very pleasant, habitualised existence or to raise my sights, live up to my capabilities and move to another job. This really made me think. I realized that I had drifted into a very routine life, which I enjoyed but was I really happy? I started to look around at other people who had been there a long time and I realized that they were in really routine lives. There was nothing particularly wrong with this but did I really want to be doing this for the rest of my life?

I decided to apply for other jobs and got one outside of the area. It wasn't long after this that I moved to another part of the country too. I am really pleased that I did as I have grown as a person, gained many more experiences and enjoyed life at levels I previously never thought possible. I do look back and reflect on Mike Norton's words. Without them would I still be in Shropshire?

Stimulus:

What is it that makes us break out of our comfortable habits and routines? All it takes is for someone or something to make you question your daily life. We all need habits and routine but we also need to question them at times. Many people appear very happy with their routine lives, but when something happens to alter the routine they are ill equipped to cope with changes. It is human nature to question your existence sometimes and unless you have tested yourself to your limits how can you ever fully know yourself?

Advice

It is a good exercise to continually reflect on your own behaviour and the activities of others. Look at what works, what doesn't, what makes people feel good and what doesn't. This kind of reflection is a real learning experience. One particularly good area to look at are the habitualised routines of you and your colleagues that stop you all from reaching your goals. Look at your actions and those of others and consider the impact that habits and attitudes have upon performance.

Positivity

Action Point

Spend some time to reflect on the habitualised routines that belong to you and your colleagues that will preclude you all from reaching your goals.

Observe the impact of habits and attitudes on performance.

Inspiration:

- **Anyone you know who decides to change their career, their life and do something totally different.**

Chapter Fourteen

Stretching Comfort Zones

Challenge yourself

'If you do what you've always done, you'll get what you've always got.'

Old adage

Learning how to change the way we think and behave is one of our most beneficial skills, because alterations in even our smallest routines can open up unforeseen routes to profound progress. By creating an environment and an attitude that allows for change, small measures act as a catalyst for larger improvements. Confront everyday habits and change them.

A change is as good as a rest.

If we behave differently we think differently.

Story

Several years ago I persuaded 13 teachers at the school I was teaching at to form a rock group to perform for the students at the end of term. This

Positivity

was pretty successful, but then we were asked to perform at a parents/students review evening along with some pretty high *calibre* student performers.

I have been through many situations where I have put myself very much outside my comfort zone. I actually actively look for situations where I can do this. However, I can safely say that on the night of the revue performance in front of 200 parents and students, I was as far most outside my comfort zone as I have ever been!

We were due to play just two songs, **'Should I stay or should I go'** and **'Rock around the clock'**. All thirteen of us were backstage waiting to go on. I looked around and every one of the band was white with fear. None of us had played to anything like this kind of audience, we had been practising for only a few weeks and if we messed up we would be ridiculed by students beyond belief! I suppose it is a little to do with the psyche of teachers as we are all programmed to give the *impression* that we are confident and in control of what we are doing. I was particularly nervous. I am a guitarist but I had volunteered to play bass guitar to fill the gap, yet this was a first time performance. Bass guitar playing is relatively straight forward you would think, but you need rhythm and you need to concentrate as you are often playing something slightly different to the main tune. Also, if you go wrong it messes up everyone. As a result of all this I was very nervous.

Steve Kenning

On stage everything went well. We were applauded off and we were even asked to perform at other functions – no doubt as a novelty act. Several of the band decided that they had been much too far out off their comfort zone and they vowed to never perform live again! The masochists amongst us decided to continue and to form a band, having all strangely enjoyed the experience.

Ten years on and the band we formed is still going strong. Now seven-piece, called *'The Moochers'*, they play about ten times a year at weddings, parties and charity events. I bowed out earlier this year in order to write and to enjoy new pleasures. Playing in a live rock band is one of the most enjoyable things you can do, yet if we hadn't collectively stretched our comfort zones all those years ago we would have missed out on hours of fun and failed to achieve something **we had all always wanted to do.**

Stimulus:

'No Officer with false teeth should attempt oral sex at zero gravity.'
Kryton, Red Dwarf

If you wear a pair of braces they make the wearing of trousers comfortable, but you probably wouldn't notice if the braces got slightly looser and if you put on a little bit of weight. Things would probably

Positivity

deteriorate over a period of time without you noticing.

If you put your thumbs inside the braces and pull the braces away from your body things become bearable but a little less comfortable, although after a while you get used to the feeling and it becomes comfortable.

However, if you stretch the braces too far and they break the elastic will snap back and hurt you.

Liken this to stretching your comfort zones. If you carry on doing what you are doing with no change then over a period of time things will probably deteriorate as you would get complacent and lazy.
If you stretch yourself slightly but not too far then you keep yourself alert to new possibilities. You also get used to a new reality that probably moves you forward.

However, if you stretch yourself too far you are likely to crash and burn with painful consequences.

The answer to a contented life, then, is to regularly move yourself forward in small jumps. Each time you move forward you create a new reality. After a period of time your new reality becomes your current reality. You will have moved forward. When you are secure in this new current reality the time is right to set yourself another small move forward. This kind of stretching of your comfort zones is remarkably successful. It stimulates, challenges and satisfies!

A good example of this is running. When you start running you might go for a mile with great difficulty and some pain. Yet after a few of these runs you start to get used to it and you feel better. Eventually you're running longer distances and feeling very good!

Advice

Everyone needs a challenge. If you feel comfortable in any aspect of your life, set yourself a new challenge before complacency sets in. If the challenge you set yourself is achievable then you have nothing to lose. The extra effort you have to put in initially is more than compensated for by the sense of achievement, the satisfaction, the feeling of excitement and the invigoration you will no doubt experience from the new challenge.

Action Point:

Look at your life. Choose one thing that you would like to improve. Set yourself a small goal that moves you forward towards your ultimate target ever so slightly. Visualise yourself achieving your goal on a regular basis. Take action to achieve your

Positivity

goal. After a period of time you will achieve your goal.

Then set yourself a new small goal that takes you closer to your ultimate target. It works!

Inspiration:

- **Richard Branson** – whatever you think of the man he is a great example of someone who is *perpetually* pushing himself outside of his comfort zone. Whenever he succeeds in one venture he embarks on another.
- **Anyone involved in extreme sports** – mountaineers are outside their comfort zones each time they *climb*. Skiing takes you out of your comfort zone on a regular basis, especially if, like me, you are a mere novice!

Chapter Fifteen

Self-talk

Your invisible friend!

'You cannot be lonely if you like the person you're alone with.'
Wayne W. Dyer

Self-talk is all about self-respect.

Self-talk is a powerful tool that can be used to shape your life anyway you want it to go. Self-talk is the process of going through things in your mind and visualising the way you want something to be. Your self-talk can be very negative. If you tell yourself in your mind that you are not very good at something then the chances are that this will become embedded in your sub-conscious and you will behave in the way you believe. If someone confirms your self-image then this makes it even more embedded. How many times do you hear someone saying, 'I can't do that?'

However, your self-talk can be an extremely positive tool for self-improvement if it is used well. To be able to fully utilise your self-talk you need to have a semblance of self-respect.

Positivity

Story

I would now like to bring to your attention the brief history of caving, in respect of my life. I have been caving once and once only. Being 6'5", caving does not register as one of my most suitable activities.

Caves are cold, damp places. You get dressed up in old boots, boiler suits and helmets and head underground into the dark. Drips of water connect with your exposed bits and you soon get covered in mud. For a while scrambling around in tunnels and coming across beautiful crystalline structures and shapes is quite exciting. However, as soon as you get stuck, your whole mood changes.

Several minutes into my first and final caving experience, a couple of smaller people ahead of me had just squeezed through a tunnel in the rock that dropped down and then up again. This made you feel as if you were arching your back as you went through the tunnel. Well that's what the other people told me. I looked at the hole by the light of my head-lamp and I really didn't fancy it. The group leader spent a good 10 minutes trying to talk me into giving it a go as the alternative was quite a long hike back.

Eventually I decided to give it a go. I squeezed myself into the hole with my arms in front of me, raised above my head. This made it very difficult to move. I was pushing with my feet and wiggling with my body. After a few minutes though my shoulders were wedged into the hole. I really couldn't move as I couldn't use my arms and my feet couldn't pull myself backwards. I really started to panic. Wiggling my whole body as much as I could and calling out for my colleagues. The leader of the group who was behind me was not much help. I could tell he was worried about the situation as his voice was quavering. A girl in front of me was far more help. She told me to lie still and calm myself. Everything would be ok.

The girl told me to close my eyes and to tell myself that I was going to get out of the tunnel in a few minutes time. She got me to visualise myself easing out of the tunnel. I spent several minutes telling myself that I could get out of the tunnel and visualising easing out of the tunnel. Then she said, 'Ready', grabbed my arms and gently pulled me forwards. I eased out of the tunnel as if there had never been a problem. I had gone into the tunnel fairly tense and came out very relaxed.

Through my self-talk and some very positive encouragement I had relaxed myself from quite a tense situation. It could have been a lot worse.

Stimulus:

The best thing about self-talk is that it is easy to do. In fact, we all do it all the time. The trick is to learn to control your self-talk and to make it work for you.

Positivity

If your self-talk is under your *control* you can achieve anything.

Advice

It is essential that you control your self-talk. There are several ways you can try to do this:

- Think carefully about what you are thinking about right now. What are you saying to yourself? Are you telling yourself that this would never work for you? NEGATIVE SELF-TALK. Or are you saying this would work for you? POSITIVE SELF-TALK. If you can read your own self-talk you can identify the negative talk and turn it into positive self-talk. That is, of course, if you really want to.
- Write down a couple of things you want to achieve. Visualise yourself doing these things and then constantly tell yourself you can do it. The power of visualisation and self-talk should help you achieve your goals, particularly if you keep looking at the things you wrote down. These will stimulate your self-talk.
- Anytime you achieve something or do something good, no matter how big or small, celebrate! Tell yourself how good you are, congratulate yourself. Make the most of your successes. Train your self-talk to be

positive and successful. If you can imprint success, positive and good thoughts into your sub-conscious then your self-talk is more likely to be positive and powerful.

Action Point

For one whole day tell yourself that you are very good at what you do. Even if some things go wrong in your day find the positives about your actions and tell yourself you are good.

Inspiration:

- **Arnold Schwarzeneggar** – in all his action movies his self-talk is unsurpassed. *Otherwise how could he do the things he does?*
- **Ian Dowie** – the former Crystal Palace football club manager. He used self-talk techniques with all his *players*. It worked, as his team over-achieved on an incredible scale for 18 months.

Chapter Sixteen

Talking to and understanding others

Respect!

'You give but little when you give of your possessions. It is when you give of yourself that you truly give.'
Kahlil Gibran

One of the key skills in life today is the ability to talk to other people. Such interpersonal skills are things that everyone considers they have but in fact very few people fully possess. Most people are incredibly poor at talking to other people. This is often because they talk without giving any consideration to the other person. Most people talk on their own terms. They don't try to understand the people they are speaking to and they often don't try to relate what they are saying to other people's situation. People in positions of responsibility are particularly poor at this. Many managers are so full of ego and self-importance that they consider themselves and themselves only. The things they say are often de-motivating and senseless. Effective managers and leaders are people who understand themselves and so don't feel the need to impose their ego on others. They understand that you need to speak to each person differently.

If you try to understand others you soon realise that everyone is different and everyone responds to different language. There are some people who need to be positively stroked all the time and fall apart if they are ever criticised in front of others. Other people like straight talking and want things said honestly and openly. If you can't recognise the difference between people, whether the people are family, friends or colleagues, then the chances are that your relationships are not going to be particularly good.

Story

There was this Managing Director of a very successful organisation. One day a colleague from a neighbouring organisation was visiting to pick up some tips and look at some of the MD's strategies that had led to success. Over coffee at the start of the day the MD was explaining how the organisation was structured when an employee burst in through the door. The *employee rushed* right up to the MD and eyeballed him. He then burst into a rant about the failings of one of the organisation's processes. The MD let the employee finish and the he calmly put his hand on his shoulder and said, *'Dennis, I can understand the way you feel but remember Rule number 6.'* The employee, Dennis, took a step back and looked

Positivity

horrified. *'Of course, oh yes, of course,'* he muttered as he shuffled out of the room.

Later in the day the visit was going well when one of the senior managers in the organisation came in to see the MD. She was very apologetic but went on to criticise the work of another senior manager and insisted that something needed to be done. The MD calmly said, *'Denise, just remember rule number 6.'* Denise went white and uttered, *'I do apologise, I'm so very sorry,'* and left the room. The visiting colleague was mystified and fascinated, especially as this happened twice more during the day.

At the end of the day, the visitor was thanking the MD for his time and openness, but he had to know one thing, *'What is rule number 6 and what were the other rules?'* The MD replied, *'There is only rule number 6 and it is very simple – don't take yourself so damn seriously!'*

Stimulus:

Too many people have too many hang-ups and because of them they feel the need to impose themselves on other people. Some people like to run people down or criticise others as they feel it helps their own self-belief. This is not the case. You raise your self-belief by being generative - by supporting and helping other people.

Steve Kenning

At my school we have changed the atmosphere of the whole organisation and made it a happier place as well as raising levels of self-esteem, partly through changing the way people talk to each other.

Staff now, mainly, talk openly about things to each other, there is very little negative whispering behind doors. People are always listened to and not ridiculed for expressing an opinion. People are also encouraged to take risks and try out new things without redress. However, it has been the way that staff talk to the students that has led to the biggest change. There are now very few staff who shout as a first course of action. Instead the language is positive. Whereas many staff used to say things like, 'You are always talking and disrupting this lesson,' they now say, ' it's not like you to disrupt a lesson you are usually really good and contribute a lot.'

The use of language is very important. If someone is regularly told that they behave in a particular way then this kind of behaviour becomes imprinted on their sub-conscious and acts as their default position. They continually revert to type. On the other hand, if you can develop a different image in someone's sub-conscious, a more positive image, then this becomes their current reality. The use of language is immensely important.

Positivity

*'If you disrespect anybody that you run into,
how in the world do you think anybody's supposed to respect you?
If you don't give a heck about the man with the bible in his hand,
just get out the way and let the gentleman do his thing.
You're the kind of gentleman that wants everything your way,
take the sheet off your face, boy, it's a brand new day.*

*Respect yourself, respect yourself.
If you don't respect yourself,
ain't nobody gonna give a good cahoots, na na na na,
respect yourself, respect yourself.*

*If you're walking round thinking that the world owes you something cause you're here.
You going out the world backwards like you did when you,
put your hand on your mouth when you cough, that'll help the solution.
Oh, you cuss around women and you don't even know their names and your dumb enough to think that'll make you a big 'ol man.'*

Staples Singers

Steve Kenning

Advice

Father Ted:

Dougal: *'Hello there Len.'*
Bishop Brennan: *'Don't call me Len. Refer to me as 'Bishop Brennan'.'*
Dougal: *'Ah right you are there Len.'*

Motivational speakers and really good coaches or leaders are all really well endowed with high quality interpersonal skills. They can make people feel good about themselves and they can motivate people to not only do things for themselves but also for the leader. We call all do this to an extent. Use third person affirmations. Sometimes when you tell someone they are really good at something it can come across as a little creepy or insincere. However, if you talk about someone positively in front of someone else you can visibly observe the object of your praise growing with delight. Praise given in front of someone else is praise with value.

Action Point:

Try to spend a whole day, yes a full 24 hours, not putting anyone down. Don't put people into a corner with your conversation and don't make people feel bad about themselves through your comments. Use the third person affirmation. As many times as possible in the day say something positive to someone in front of another person.

Positivity

Inspiration:

- **Sheila Hancock**: The actress. As Sheila Hancock says, *'To tell someone they're potentially wonderful when all they've ever heard is that they're worthless is a very powerful thing.'* She also re-counts a part she played on film with Bette Davis. One day at the end of a scene Sheila couldn't help but say, *'Miss Davis, you were wonderful.'* She was so genuinely, obviously touched, which shook me; replying, 'Why, thank you, honey. Normally, the highest praise I get is, 'Print 1! It's a wrap'.' Sheila thought to herself, *'My god, she's taken on the Hollywood studios and won, but no-one ever tells her that she's good. She's so vulnerable, despite the tough façade.'* This only increased Sheila's belief that in telling someone when you appreciate them, or when you think *what they do is really good*.

Chapter Seventeen

Taking Risks

Scaring yourself silly!

'My persistence is my measure of my belief in myself.'
Ian Gilbert

We are moving into a time period where creativity will be the most prized of attributes. The ability to take inspiration and make new things happen will become the expectation of anyone looking for success.

We are not all risk takers though. Why is this? Is it genetic? Is it conditioning? Or is it to do with our self-belief? There are undoubtedly many factors that help create a personality. However risk-taking is essentially born out of self-belief, even if the self-belief is misplaced and reckless at times.

All of us have had important crossroads in our lives. Times, when we have had to make a decision. What did you do? Did you take the safe option or did you take the risky open-ended option?

If you took the safe option you probably wonder what your life might be like had you taken the risk.

Positivity

You are probably not that happy with your life and suffer from regrets and you may well blame other people for what is wrong with your life.

Whereas if you had taken responsibility for your own life and taken a risk life would have been very different and probably much better! On the other hand, having taken the risky route there is no doubt that your life will have been interesting, but perhaps not always good, yet you would have few regrets, only maybe wishing you had not been so foolhardy! You would have learnt a lot about yourself, stretched yourself and experienced things you might not have otherwise. Also, you would not be blaming others for your misfortunes.

In my life I have taken many risks and they have led to things I could have never imagined. I have been lucky, or has it been skill? As I have not regretted any of the risks I have taken. This is, I think, because every risk I have taken has been a calculated risk. I have always had a fall-back position.

I have also, at times, taken the easy route and not taken a risk. Often the fact that I had not taken the risk would eat away at me and over a period of time and I would eventually convince myself that I should take the risk and go for it. There have been times too when I have become quite unhappy because to take a risk, even though I felt it would be the right thing to do, would be uncomfortable for other people in my life. This hasn't always stopped me but it has led to a lot of hard work convincing others to go along with the risk.

Story

Risk is a very personal thing but it is essential if you are to achieve a fulfilling life whilst you are on this planet. However, risk taking is a real art. A risk that is unplanned and not rehearsed is a foolish one.

Two colleagues I have worked with recently both took a very similar risk, but the outcomes were very different.

Belinda Moore was a senior administrator at one of the schools I worked at for a very long time. Belinda and her husband Phil, a bricklayer, were very adaptable, gregarious people; they enjoyed life in their own way to the full. Their children were grown up and settled, one son was in Australia. In their mid-fifties they decided to try a new life themselves in Australia. They visited an area where they had friends on several occasions, found a new development, picked a property that would take a couple of years to build and started to plan their new life. They sold their house in England and lived in rented property for a year. During this time they visited Australia a couple of times, sorting out work and fixing up places to stay while their property was being built. Two years ago they

Positivity

moved to Australia and although their new house is yet to be finished they are having a wonderful time.

Belinda and Phil took a great risk – changing their lifestyle totally. Their life in England was good, yet they wanted to experience something different. They were not running away from anything. They also planned very carefully and had contingencies for virtually every situation.

The other colleague who moved to Bulgaria was a guy I will call Alan to preserve any embarrassment. Alan and I worked very closely together as he was a senior manager. We had a very good working relationship. We got to know each other well and over the years I had learned that he wanted to try his hand at life in the developing economy of Bulgaria. He was a little stressed out with his job, although he performed well at it and was doing a good job. I sensed that his wife, a linguist, was unhappy and wanted more. Alan gave the impression of someone searching for the better life that doesn't exist. He also had two young children.

Alan, with many talents, was offered a new role at his school, a role that fully utilised his talents, was less stress inducing and was promotion. He turned it down. Instead he resigned and said his family were moving to Bulgaria to start up a watersports initiative, a language school or to do up properties. Alan and his wife had sold their house and were off to the fairly unspoilt region of Bulgaria on the Black Sea. Alan and his wife visited the area only once before they went, knew no-one out there and, just before they went, their house sale in this country fell through. They went to Bulgaria, lived in a caravan, sent their kids to a local school and returned to Britain three months later. Alan's wife missed her extended family, they couldn't find enough work and they couldn't find a suitable property to rent or buy. Alan is now working as a main scale teacher in a local school earning half the salary he was earning before he left.

Alan and his wife did little risk analysis and did not appear to have had a back-up plan. They also, or so it seems, went for the wrong reasons. The best risks are taken from a position of strength, when you know yourself and are confident with your life and anything life can throw at you.

Stimulus:

Risks should always be calculated risks. I once spoke to Michael Barber, then the Head of the Government Policy Unit, at a conference. We talked briefly about risks and how essential they are. He thought that it was good to be continually out of your comfort zone through taking risks, and that there had been times in his life that he had been scared all the time. I'm not sure if this is the way to do it. There have been many times when I have taken a risk and it has led to something I hadn't foreseen and as a result I had spent a few sleepless nights wondering what I had done! Yet

Positivity

every time I knew that the worst-case scenario would not be too bad as I had already planned for failure of the risk. When I take a risk I always know what I will do if it doesn't work. However, I also only take risks that I believe will work, and they invariably do pay off.

Imagine yourself stuck in a log cabin surrounded by snow. Food running low. Would you stay put and hope to be rescued? Or would you take a risk and head for the town 10 miles away? I would certainly head for the town. I would be very confident of succeeding, as I would build the risk little by little and think through each stage of it analysing potential problems and finding solutions. I would also be very clear of the objective and visualise the success of my risk.

Advice

For risks to work:
- *They must be your own, not forced upon you by someone else.*
- *You must believe that the risk is achievable.*
- *The risk must be to improve things, not just to change something for the sake of change.*
- *The risk must be well planned.*
- *The risk must be calculated.*

Action Point:

If you are not a *natural risk* taker try something on a small scale. For example:
- *Do your weekly shopping on a different day, in a different supermarket*
- *If you are unattached ask the person to dinner who you really most like (who is also unattached).*
- *Buy yourself some clothes that you would love to wear but would normally never dare to, and then wear them!*
- *Surprise your partner with an unexpected romantic treat.*

Whatever risk you take, plan it out. Visualise it working many, many times. Also, plan each stage of the risk and work out what you would do if at any stage things go wrong. Then do it!

Inspiration:

Eddie 'The Eagle' Edwards – back in the eighties and nineties Britain had its very own ski jumper. Eddie *persistently* risked his neck with jump after jump. With each jump he became more and more famous resulting in a life more interesting and varied than he could have ever had imagined. He took the risk to get involved in ski jumping and it *paid off.*

Chapter Eighteen

Setting the Climate

Global Warming

'The glory of friendship is not the outstretched hand, nor the kindly smile nor the joy of companionship; it is the spiritual inspiration that comes to one when he discovers that someone else believes in him and is willing to trust him.'

Ralph Waldo Emerson

One of the most fundamental elements of successful people or organisations is the climate they create. Successful people create a positive climate around them that motivates people and makes others feel good. Note: Some people operate by fear and appear to be successful, but they are not. Successful people are people who know themselves, are comfortable and confident with their own skin and are generative towards others. Successful organisations are where people feel trusted, empowered and challenged.

How do you create the right kind of positive climate around yourself or in your organisation?

Steve Kenning

- Know what you want to achieve – have a vision for how you want yourself or your organisation to operate.
- Have clear values that you do not compromise.
- Value, trust, encourage and challenge people.
- Develop a framework for action – the 8 conditions are useful here:
    - Belonging – involve people.
    - Heroes – act as an inspiration.
    - SENSE OF ACCOMPLISHMENT - encourage people to feel good about their achievements.
    - FUN AND EXCITEMENT – have a laugh and challenge people.
    - CURIOSITY AND CREATIVITY - make life interesting.
    - SPIRIT OF ADVENTURE - take risks.
    - LEADERSHIP AND RESPONSIBILTY – lead by example.
    - CONFIDENCE TO TAKE ACTION - believe in yourself.

Story

Many years ago I worked at a school in Shropshire. It was in the most beautiful location but was the most appallingly run school. The Headteacher was a weak woman who constantly questioned everything everyone did, wanted no fun or

Positivity

excitement in the school and utterly failed as a leader. I had only been teaching for a couple of years but after a couple of weeks I realised that in this school I was by myself. I had a total lack of respect for the Head, particularly after she came into one of my lessons and told me off in front of the class for having laughter emanating from the room! The Head was also regularly undermined by a very effective Deputy Head.

The climate the Head created because of her leadership was one of a total lack of respect for anyone. The students didn't respect authority and the staff didn't respect authority. If you were a good teacher you survived but the vast majority of teachers did their own thing.

Staff meetings were hilarious. There was a large betting school amongst the staff, developed mainly to bring some lightness to a depressing organisation, and some staff would bet on anything. Staff meetings were not, from the staff view, focussed on education or management issues, instead they were focussed on competitions. My favourite was the based around how many types of something you could mention out load as part of the meeting without being reprimanded. The most memorable was animals, probably because I won the £20 kitty. Comments such as, 'The students move around the school like herds of elephants', commenting on breaking up a fight, then I said, 'they were rutting like a couple of deer, I had to use bear like strength to separate them…but they went

Steve Kenning

off to the Deputy Heads office like a couple of shamed whippets with their tails between their legs.' I feel quite ashamed about behaving like this now, but the culture and climate created by the Headteacher encouraged such behaviour. I hated the place and moved on after 18 months in the school. Shortly after I left there was a vote of no confidence in the Headteacher and she was removed. It wasn't long before the school was operating very effectively, but with a very different climate.

Stimulus:

It is quite easy to create a climate. Consider the different atmosphere at a football match between the usual hubbub and when there is a well respected one minute silence. I am always moved when more than 30,000 people stand in silence as a mark of respect.

The best vision for a climate for an organisation is one where people feel safe, trusted, challenged, and where there are high expectations and high aspirations. People have to feel comfortable in the place they work, yet at the same time there need to be high expectations. These can only be created by setting up the right systems, by developing people, by constantly stroking the system, and by gently moving the place forward.

What climate do you want to create for yourself?

Positivity

This really is a little like creating an aura. I remember once having a conversation in Brighton with a clairvoyant. We were sitting on the side of the street looking at people rushing by. He told me he could see four or five different coloured auras encircling people. Some were very vibrant; these mainly belonged to people who looked happy and full of life. Others had grey auras and surrounded miserable looking people.

There are certain people you want to be with and others you can't stand to be around. Why is this? Could it be because of their auras?

Advice

The basic rule to creating a positive climate around yourself is to, **'treat others as you would wish to be treated yourself.'**

If you feel good about yourself, are happy with who you are and are continually trying to better yourself in the way you treat others then you will start to emanate positivity and other people will feel comfortable around you. Some people are all over other people with praise, but if it is purely done for their own gain then such behaviour is transparent. Also, some people are so lacking in self-esteem that they mistrust and run down people who are nice to them. Don't let such attitude deter you from your path. Such people would love to have ammunition to use against you in the shape of evidence of you having been unpleasant or spiteful towards someone.

Action Point:

Spend the next week treating others as you would want to be treated yourself. Don't be put off by people's attitude towards you, stick to your guns!

Inspiration:

- **Tesco** – compared to other supermarkets they always seem to have the edge on the climate most of their stores emanate. Good value, without being cheap, quality, **good service**.
- **Sue Campbell** – President of the Youth Sports Trust and adviser to the government on school sports. Sue is the kind of person who makes you feel really good about yourself. She is incredibly busy, yet she has time for everyone. She undoubtedly has an ego, yet it doesn't get in the way of who she is.

Chapter Nineteen

Can You Feel the Force?

Set up your radar devices!

'Your work is to discover your world and then with all your heart give yourself to it.'

The Buddha

I spent a long period of my twenties fascinated by the North American Indian culture. This started when I worked on a summer camp in the USA. The camp in Minnesota was in the heart of Indian country and I regularly passed through reservations during canoe trips. There was a student on the camp who taught Indian Studies and he filled my head with a real awe for what seemed to be a majestic people with a real affinity, not only with nature, but also with themselves.

There are a lot of writings about the thoughts of North American Indian leaders. They make fascinating reading. The more enlightened ones actually foresaw the end of their race in visions and dreams. To do this they used the same 'sixth sense' that their people had used to hunt and survive in often harsh natural situations.

Steve Kenning

This ability to see ahead is probably about little more than people who really understood themselves, who were in tune with their life and surroundings, who took the time and were relaxed enough to really consider the signs of a changing world. This skill is something the western world has generally lost. There is very little inner peace in people and people generally do not know themselves.

The ability to 'feel the force', to be able to read the signs of what is likely to happen is an essential feature of successful people in personal and work life. In the work place if you can read what the market place or competitors, are going to do you can make important decisions to your benefit. In your personal life you can read other people and see situations coming then life can be far easier to manage.

Story

Large organisations fascinate me. *How does a company like Glaxo Smith-Kline operate on such a scale and stay successful? How have Orange managed to get such a good hold on the mobile phone market in Britain. And why don't they just re-name chewing gum Wrigleys in honour of their totally mastery of the product?*

Some organisations are destined to die. From afar anyone can see the signs, but *how is it that they*

Positivity

can't? It is often this lack of awareness to read the signs, to see the future, to understand what is happening outside the doors of the organisation. A classic example is the County Council. The County Council is probably the most inept organisation in existence. No doubt there are some examples of good practice and there are undoubtedly some good people working for them but on the whole they are superb examples of how not to operate an organisation. They are full of people unwilling or unable to make a decision, moribund by bureaucracy and duplication, managed by small minded people unwilling to take risks, and incapable of understanding what the people they are supposed to represent want. Like other organisations in the latter stages of their life, they seem unable or unwilling to change, yet without change they will not survive. Even when new leadership and new ideas are introduced, often the malaise is so deeply rooted in the organisation that it continues on its road to oblivion. (What a fantastic word that is!). County Councils also replace their retiring officers with officers they often know, because it is safe, and they are governed by county Councillors! This is the real fag-end of democracy. Anyone who wants to could be a county councillor, there is hardly a surfeit of people willing to put themselves forward for this role. Why then do they wield such power over our finances and our lives? Answers on the back of a matchstick please!

Steve Kenning

One story of the ineptness of a county council is related to one in the North-East which was faced, as is a regular occurrence, with a need to cut costs. One suggestion, from a learned officer, was to turn the cats eyes off at night! Bizarre, but true.

Operating on the same lines is a well-known British airline. We went to Oslo on this airline a few weeks ago and although we fly a lot, mainly on the budget airlines, I can safely say that this British airline gave a very good impression of a dispractic organisation, unable to co-ordinate the actions of its separate parts. This catalogue of incompetence was hilarious:

- We checked in electronically 12 hours before we had to board, as instructed on the website and selected our seats. This meant staying up until past midnight. Arriving at Heathrow we went to the fast check-in and used to computers to confirm our bookings. No chance, this machine failed miserably to find us and so we had to go to the check-in desk.
- At the check-in desk we were told that the baggage conveyor wasn't working and so there were massive queues and our bags would have to be taken by porter. This didn't fill us with any great confidence as the porter disappeared with our trolley without any real idea where he was heading.
- We got on the plane half an hour late. An hour later we were still sitting on the plane, but no-one had told us why. Eventually the

Positivity

pilot tried to tell us why, apparently the automated baggage loading machine had broken and they couldn't move it out of the way in order to utilise another. Eventually we took off.
- Reaching our destination, Oslo, we were not surprised to find out that one of our bags had not been put on the plane and was in fact, still in London.

What made all this worse was that at every point there seemed to be no one willing to take responsibility to tell us what was happening, to apologise or even to make things happen. The classic example of an organisation too large and complacent to react to its customers' needs or to any operational problems.

Stimulus:

As a manager of a large organisation I have always tried to read the future. On a large scale to be able to act pro-actively and to make things happen before they happen to you. It has always been better to get there first and have the ability to influence the way things are shaped as opposed to waiting for something to be done to you. On a more local scale I have always tried to read the behaviour of people with a view to managing the organisation.

To read people, to listen, to observe their behaviour gives you an idea of how new initiatives are bedding down and, in particular, how the climate of the organisation is developing. In the early days of shaping the climate of the organisation I would hear that someone was unhappy or being negative about what was going on. I would go straight to see them and find out their issues and talk them round. The purpose of this was to prevent any negativity and to bring any discontent out into the open. What I didn't want was an organisation where people were talking behind closed doors.

Advice:

Take time to *watch, observe, look, hear, listen, see, feel and touch* everything and everyone. (Hugging should be seriously considered before you engage in it. As Headteacher my school made the national press for discouraging students from unnecessary hugging in case it gave out the wrong signals!) Read the signals, monitor what is going on around you. React and adjust to the things that affect you. This takes some skill, as you need to learn to read what is important and what needs to be ignored. The operation of your Reticular Activating System (RAS) is essential here. This highlights the things that are important to you. Learn to listen to your RAS. Also, learn to react, don't sit back if your gut feeling is to do something about the messages you are receiving. If you pick things up on your radar then you are picking up warning signals, you then need to act.

Positivity

Action Point:

Find five minutes at work to do nothing but look and listen. Watch other people and listen to what they are saying. Try to be a fly on the wall. You should pick up a great deal of information even in this short period of time. Take one snippet of information and act upon it. Try it!

Inspiration:

- **Neo** – the part Keanu Reeves plays in the film The Matrix. It's amazing how **Neo** has the time to see everything that is thrown at him – bullets, bodies, etc. We are led to believe that it is **Neo's** ability to control his mind that enables this to happen. Something to strive for!

Steve Kenning

Chapter Twenty

Making Things Happen

Plan, talk, massage, talk, massage, etc.

'A person's life is not measured in the amount of money made or time spent, nor is it measured in its length. A life is measured in its hopes, dreams, and its ability to make them happen.'

Author Unknown

As a great believer in the premise that if you put your mind to it, you can do anything, I find it quite hard to admit that THERE ARE SOME THINGS THAT I JUST CANNOT DO. For example:

- On the small Dash aircraft of Air South-West that fly from Plymouth to Gatwick, as a 6'5" male, standing up to pee into the aircraft toilet is a virtual impossibility
- Getting my seventeen year old son to converse on a regular basis in more than mono-syllabic grunts
- Willing Aston Villa to win the Premiership, although Martin O'Neill, the manager, is certainly helping this vision.

Positivity

- Finding anything worth eating in a popular American fast-food burger restaurant???

However, you can make a great many things happen with the right attitude, the right approach and a firm belief that you will achieve what you set out to achieve.

Father Ted:

Father Jack: *'Don't tell me I'm still on that feckin' island.'*

Story:

There is an excellent American advert for Reebok. Terry Tate, a linebacker in American football, is a huge guy who is used to charging at people and bringing them down hard. In the advert he is used by a company to motivate the workers in an office complex. Terry's motivational techniques are coercive – people work through fear. The short advert shows Terry hard at work tackling ANYBODY WHO IS NOT GIVING THE COMPANY 100%. This is a common technique for getting things done – build a climate of fear.

Stimulus:

To get anything done well, you need to get people to want to do things. Only then do you not only get things done but you get things done to a high standard. The key is to invest in people.

There are several key things you must do if you are to make things happen around you:

- Massage people – their vanity, their egos, their productivity, their successes.
- Set short term targets and time targets to inch things forward towards the end result.
- Work hard at getting the thing done, this will create luck.
- Know what you want to achieve.
- Practice, practice, practice.

To get things done by other people is particularly hard.

Advice

One key element of getting things done is to realise that we all have little blindspots, called scotomas, that limit our ability to achieve some things. If you have ever lost something, like your glasses or car keys, and have looked everywhere for them before you find them staring at you in a place you have already looked, then you have had a scotoma. Sometimes we can't see for looking. If something isn't in the place we expect it to be, or if it is in a different context, we sometimes don't see it.

People who lead very repetitive and routine lives are particularly prone to scotomas, as their minds

Positivity

are not trained to see the unexpected. Scotomas do stop us from achieving things. The key to avoiding scotomas is to keep your mind fresh and alert, always seeking and open to new experiences.

To make things happen you also have to get people to believe that they have limitless potential and that anything is possible. This is a big task. You set about it over a period of time by trying to change their current reality:

- Tell them continually that they are better than they think they are.
- Help them to visualise achieving small tasks.
- Perform third person affirmations on them.
- Praise them regularly.

People with high levels of self-efficacy find it relatively easy to make things happen. The difficulty is to develop self-efficacy in other people. People with high levels of self-efficacy:

- See most things as a challenge
- Set themselves challenging goals and stick to the task
- Use self-analysis to keep them on task
- Heighten their effort in the face of setbacks
- Consider failure to be due to a lack of effort or due to non-conducive circumstances
- Rarely get stressed or depressed.

Action Point:

Choose a work colleague randomly, or a friend, and test your skills of efficacy out on them. Think of a task you would like them to do for you. Try to build up their efficacy and their self-belief enough over a period of time in order to get them to do something you want them to do for you. When the moment is ready try it out, see if the effort was worth it.

Inspiration:

- **Women** – women are highly *skilled* at getting men to do things for them. If you're a man, watch, observe, learn and admire!

Chapter Twenty-One

Convincing people you are right

Are you believable?

'Whether you think you can or you think you can't, you're probably right.'
Henry Ford

Some people are so convinced that they are always right that they don't even bother to listen to other people's views. We all know and intensely dislike people who behave in such a way. The problem for most of the rest of us is this: Unless you are a supremely arrogant and an ignorant know-it-all you probably lack the full confidence to persuade others that you really do know what you are talking about. This takes me back to school when occasionally the really smart kids who always gave very confident sounding answers occasionally said something you definitely knew was wrong. Did you shout out the right answer? – Noooo, you just kept quiet as you lacked the confidence to say anything. It's the same in a team pub quiz. If you're playing with someone who is so anally retentive they swot up on dictionaries, but on one question you know the answer but they are convinced that they are right with their answer. You give in because you can't be bothered to push it. However, you feel a great sense of inner triumph when you do actually get it right!

Sometimes you know the answer, you know the best way to do something, you know which way things should go. But how do you get others to go along with you?

Story

I was in the states a couple of years ago on a research visit with about ten colleagues. One of them, John, who I worked closely with, was good company and we enjoyed our non-working hours together in Boston where we were based. John was a real charmer with the opposite sex, or at least he thought he was. It's always quite amusing to take the part of a slightly detached observer watching a male who is convinced he resembles Steve McQueen and is irresistible to women, go to work on the opposite sex. As you watch his routine you notice that he is so convinced that he is so right and so much in touch with the people he is working on that he misses all the important signals. John was forever saying that he was getting on great with some woman and then something would happen to spoil things at the last minute. What he failed to realise that the poor woman was always trying to find a way out, he always missed the despairing glances and the cries for help in the women's eyes.

Positivity

John did have the confidence of someone who believed he was right and, to be fair, with a certain type of woman he did succeed. I remember one night, we wanted to dance and we were in deepest Maine in a city called Bangor. Our American hosts took us to the Ramada Hotel, about the only place where there was any kind of nightlife. Tonight though there was a disco. It was full of rednecks and the place stank of trouble. We felt safe as we had a couple of our rugby playing colleagues with us who were enormous!

The night moved on and John had a few drinks and a few dances. He was slowly eyeing up the women on the dance floor, looking for the prettiest. We managed to steer him away from a couple that had particularly homicidal looking boyfriends, until he finally focussed on a group of three women, two who were really quite gorgeous. John grooved over to them and spent the next twenty-minutes oozing confidence and charm to these two women. Credit to him, he was working hard. As the women laughed and danced with him his confidence grew and he stepped up the pace. Just as you sensed he was going in for the kill the two really georgeous looking women grabbed each other and started kissing in a very sensual way. The look of realisation on John's face was hilarious to the rest of us, as you could see his deflation and dejection as he realised that he had been trying to chat up two lesbians.

This moral of this story is that however much you convince yourself you're right, it's a lot harder to convince others.

Stimulus:

Father Ted: *'I think it might work, Dougal. I know it'll work. It will work.'*
Dougal: *'It won't work will it Ted?'*
Father Ted: *'....It won't, no.'*

So convincing yourself that you are right is relatively straightforward, but *how do you convince others?* Some people seem to have friends who would do anything for them, others have work colleagues who would almost appear to die for their boss. *What qualities do these people have?* Often the difference between developing real loyalty in friends and having people who really believe in you at work is quite marked, although there are similarities. With friendship the key factors are:

- **Loyalty** – essential to real friendships.
- **Honesty** – trust.
- **Interest in others** – a respect and interest in other people's life gives value and raises self-esteem in others.
- **Drive and a clear idea of where you are going** – people like to be around people who make things happen.
- **Shared values** – friendships are built around common values.

Positivity

- **Positivity** – no-one wants to be with someone who is persistently negative.

In the workplace the same kind of factors are important, although for different reasons:

- *Drive, ambition and success* – people like to know where they are going, what the future holds and they want to be associated with success.
- *Respect and value* – people work for people who value them and respect their contribution.
- *Fairness* – nobody likes an uneven playing field where there appears to be favouritism.
- *Firmness and high expectations* – people like to work for someone who is consistently pushing them and others forward and does not tolerate any inefficiency.
- *Lead by example* – people respect someone who experiences what they experience.

Advice

If you really want to get people to believe in you and to respond to your wishes, whether in your work life or your private life, then there are basically two things you have to do:

1. **Develop an element of personal mastery**. You need to get beyond the point where you are continually using other

people to build your own self-worth or to massage your ego. Other people really respond to people who appear confident, self-contained and, in particular, who know who they are, what they want and where they are going.
2. **Develop your understanding and awareness of other people and then utilise your interpersonal skills.** Everyone is different and everyone needs different handling. Anyone can be motivated with the right level of support, guidance and encouragement.

Action Point:

Use your self-talk to build your confidence and self-esteem, make every effort not to use other people for this purpose. Refrain from telling stories about how good you are, what wonderful things you did over the weekend, and looking to draw out positive statements about you from people. Instead try to develop a very friendly aloofness in terms of yourself. Don't give much away about yourself but spend as much time as possible asking about other people and encouraging them. Over a period of time, this kind of approach, coupled with a directness and positiveness in your behaviour, should increase your credibility.

Positivity

Inspiration:

- **Tim Brighouse** – former Chief Education Officer of Birmingham, one-man education *think-tank* and presently transforming the education of London's schools. Anyone involved in education believes everything this man says. He speaks sense, he speaks plainly and he speaks from the heart.

Chapter Twenty-Two

Changing your mind

We all make mistakes

A big failure of western culture over he past couple of centuries has been its intolerance of mistakes. The quest for success and advancement has meant that people have been chastised, punished and, as a result, afraid to make mistakes. Today, **things are changing**. There is a realisation that to make mistakes is good. A risk-taking culture where people test things out, learn from mistakes, but also reach levels more cautious people can only dream about, is being encouraged in many organisations. The acceptance is growing that in order to be truly creative you have got to take risks. To make mistakes is OK. It's also good practice to accept and acknowledge that you have made a mistake.

Story

When I first became Headteacher, the school I took over was a 'stuck' school. It was doing OK, but despite potential, nothing was moving forward. I decided early on that the best course of action was to get all the staff together to talk about any issues and to chart the way forward together. In my

Positivity

naivety I thought people would use the opportunity to come together under one vision. The problem was that I did this a couple of weeks into my Headship and I hadn't developed the culture to make such an activity work or even assessed the risks.

As it turned out the event, in the slightly longer term was one of the best moves I made, as it cleared out a lot of issues from the past. Immediately though, it was a disaster. A lot of the staff used the opportunity to have a real go at the senior managers of the school, all of whom had a dreadful evening. It took me several weeks to build up my relationships with them, to repair relationships between them and the staff and to re-construct their self-belief.

I acknowledged my naivety to the senior staff for encouraging the meeting and apologised for the event. At the time it was the wrong course of action and a mistake on my part. However, after a couple of months the culture and ethos of the organisation was transformed. I doubt if the organisation would have developed in quite the same way or quite as quickly without that initial meeting.

Stimulus:

A mistake is something that is done in error, where something goes wrong. A mistake is only a real problem if you come to regret it. From a very early age we learn through our mistakes. Most of us only talk complete rubbish for the first few years of our life, although some people never seem to progress much further for the rest of their lives! As parents we generally encourage our children to keep trying and eventually they'll stop making mistakes – they will stop falling off their bike, they will learn to eat with a knife and fork, and so on. Why then do we always expect adults to always get things right? We keep learning until the day we die, so why should we reach the magic age of say, eighteen, and suddenly become experts at everything?

We are also so governed by this culture of having to be successful that many people lack the self-confidence to admit they have made a mistake.

Advice

Whenever you do something wrong, take a risk, admit to your mistake. First of all analyse your mistake, be fully aware of why you made the mistake and the full implications of it. Make sure you have thought about the rescue strategy – how are you going to put the mistake right? Also, assess how people will react if you admit to the mistake. Having done all this and you believe that all damage limitation strategies are in place, admit your mistake. People will, over time, get used to this strategy and respect you for your honesty.

Positivity

Action Point:

Over the next few weeks look out for other people making mistakes. Don't comment on them or highlight them but observe how people manage themselves. *Do they cover up and try to pretend nothing has happened? Do they blame someone else? Or do they take responsibility?* Watch and learn. Take your pick of the strategies that people use that are the best – no doubt it will mainly be those of the people who admit to their mistakes.

Inspiration:

- **Georgie Manson** – one of my Personal Assistants at one of my schools. Georgie worked extremely hard and was put under **pressure** everyday. She was extremely effective at what she did and she did everything with a smile. Working under such pressure she made some mistakes, yet she always, without fail, took responsibility, repaired any *damage* and moved on.

Chapter Twenty-Three

Building Confidence

Making people feel safe

'Tell me and I'll forget; show me and I may remember; involve me and I'll understand.'

Chinese Proverb

A real key to being a positive influence on the life of other people is the desire to want to make other people feel good about themselves. If you generally feel like this then, if there is a heaven, I am sure you will be welcomed! People who enjoy making other people feel good about themselves are generally people who feel good about themselves. The exact converse is also true of course. There are many people with unhappy little lives and low self-esteem who delight in other people's misery and appear to get pleasure from making other people feel bad.

People can take advantage of nice people though, so the key to making this work – being a really nice person, making others feel good about themselves, getting people to work for you and ensuring that people don't take advantage of your niceness – is to develop strategies that not only make people feel

Positivity

good but also create certain expectations for the way they behave around you. Easy!

Story

A senior colleague once commented on my management style, which I think was a compliment. However it was meant it has stuck with me and it has become a very definite and successful feature of my leadership character. What this colleague said was that when I had to criticise or discipline someone I followed a particular pattern:

- I did not ever criticise the person in public.
- I did not ever put them into a corner, leaving them with nowhere to salvage any self-respect.
- I always said what I had to say with a smile.

My colleague, who had observed me for some time, felt that this style was very effective in that people knew they had been censured but as it was done with a smile there was no confrontation and they escaped with some visible dignity, however they might be feeling inside.

Whatever your character and however good your interpersonal skills, you still get it wrong quite often, but if you try, you get it right more often than not. Also, if you do try people start to trust you and feel safe with you. They have confidence in you.

Steve Kenning

A friend of mine, Russ Quaglia, Director of the Global Institute for Raising Student Aspirations in the USA, was visiting Cornwall. We were staying at the Headland Hotel in Newquay and one night a few of us decided to go to a restaurant about a mile down the coast. We got a taxi there but decided to walk back. It was about 10 p.m and very dark.

Russ had great confidence in me and my colleagues as we had set up some good links in this country for him. Here was a man in his late forties, with dodgy knees, in a strange country, who was about to cross a very rough beach in the dark. Russ had such faith in us that he did not question our route. Half an hour and a twisted ankle later, and plenty of expletives, our little group emerged from the beach and giggled about our little adventure over a few drinks in the bar.

Stimulus:

'We are each of us angels with only one wing, and we can only fly by embracing one another.'

Luciano de Crescenzo

The key to building confidence in people is to respect and value them. It is very difficult to achieve anything alone anymore. Even a successful marathon runner utilises coaches, nutritionists and a team of other support workers. It is very

Positivity

important to value the contributions of everyone you work and socialise with if you want to make the most of your life. If you are positive with the people in your life, then they are going to feel better about themselves and achieve in lots of ways.

Advice

Build you own confidence by being strong, supportive and positive towards other people. If you do this without fail you will not only gain their confidence, you will make them feel safe with you and you will reap the benefits. You must avoid flashes of unpredictability, particularly if this involves you being moody or losing your temper.

Action Point:

This action point is *really important*.

Become more aware of:
- *how you speak to other people*
- *your body language in the presence of other people*
- *your moods*
- *your temper*
- *your attitude towards others.*

Be positive in every **respect**. If you can be positive in the way you behave towards other people you will notice a real transformation in their attitude and relationship towards you.

Inspiration:

- **My 14 year old daughter, Tess**. When she is a bundle of fun and energy, which is most of the time, she is so nice to people they immediately feel good.

Chapter Twenty-Four

There are no rules

I did it my way!

'Do not follow where the path may lead. Go instead where there is no path and leave a trail.'

Ralph Waldo Emerson

The future is in the hands of the intelligent rule breaker. Although we need written rules and statute laws to guide our actions and to maintain a society that is tolerable to live in, we need to push the boundaries of our existence that are defined by infinite, unwritten rules, relating to behaviour, actions and virtually every aspect of the way we live. It is these unwritten rules that make life miserable for some and that limit our creativity and enjoyment of life.

Develop an attitude that you are not going to live your life by someone else's unwritten rules and instead you are going to search and discover a *better way*, then you will almost certainly be fulfilled, as opposed to frustrated.

Steve Kenning

Story

Some years ago I took a couple of mini-bus loads of Sixth-Form students to Nuremberg in Germany. At this time, Nuremberg was still in West Germany and, as it was very close to East Germany, we went and had a look at the border, with its guard towers and guard dogs – very spooky it was too! The visit was really a cultural one. Our contact took us backstage to the Opera, to various museums and churches, and to fantastic vineyards for wine tasting.

On our second visit, the Berlin Wall had come down and the Czech border was open. As a result, we had a quick vote and decided to drive the five hours to Prague one day. It was fascinating entering Czechoslovakia just a few weeks after the border had come down and was opened up to the west. Arriving in Prague was an experience in itself. Few of the traffic lights seemed to work, making progress through the city complete guesswork. We went into a multi-storey car park where there were so few lights that the roof rack of the mini-bus got caught on some unseen pipes hanging from the roof. The scary noise and falling dust arising from this incident made us hurry to another parking area.

The students had given me the money they wanted to spend for me to change at one of the official currency conversion centres. We were queuing waiting to exchange our Marks when a Czech male

Positivity

came up to me and asked if I wanted a better rate. The rate he was quoting was massively better. So, I broke the rules and went to the rear of the office we were in and exchanged our Marks.

By the time we returned to Germany we had had eaten three meals, bought lots of gifts and been ripped off. Yet, after officially exchanging our remaining money back into Marks, we still had the same amount of money that we originally started with! Challenging the unwritten rules had gained us all a great deal and I managed to live with my conscience!

This is perhaps a slightly risky example of breaking the rules. However, in everyday life there are many unwritten rules you can break.

Stimulus:

Father Ted: *'You know the phrase 'to take care of something?' Well I realise now that you meant that in a sort of Al Pacino way. Whereas I was thinking more along the lines of Julie Andrews.'*

To remain fully positive and to succeed in life you need to live by your own rules. This does not mean that you should break rules to the detriment of other people. Breaking unwritten rules is fine if it doesn't directly affect other people. Breaking unwritten rules keeps you alive mentally, as it challenges you to discover new ways of doing things.

Steve Kenning

Have you ever wanted to:

- Wear something very smart but very different to a formal dinner?
- Wear your hair different to expectations.
- Dance flamboyantly.
- Call your boss by their first name if they are usually addressed as Sir.
- Go blebleblelbleblllllllll when the going gets tough!

In your private life try to be a little bit different. Other people find the unusual exciting. The key is to be unusual and different without appearing to be a complete jerk, or to be irritating or to be scary. The easiest way to be different is to slightly bend those unwritten rules that most of us follow as we often lack the confidence to challenge them.

Advice

Life is a journey of discovery. Although we actually spend much of our life behaving in a way that others expect us to behave. This is fine as long as it doesn't constrain us or make us unhappy. We all have the adolescent in us. In fact it never really leaves us. We all feel seventeen in our heads, even when we are in our fifties, the trouble is we also learn to behave according to expectations. We get societised. Real adolescents rebel against the unwritten rules imposed upon them by their parents, for a few years they break free, before

Positivity

getting conditioned by society and behaving according to expectations.

We all need to recapture the energy and zest for life of our adolescence. Adolescents lack the experience to know what to do with the discoveries they make from challenging the rules. Just imagine what you could achieve if as a thirty, forty, fifty or even sixty year old, you used your experience to guide and develop an adolescent like disregard for the untouchable aspects of our society.

Action Point:

Break some unwritten rules. Don't always behave according to other people's expectations. Do your own thing, live your own life, as long as you don't hurt others. Just do it!

Inspiration:

- **The people behind the low-cost airlines, Easyjet, Ryanair,etc** – They have all taken on an established field, the airline industry, and reinvented the rules of operation.

Chapter Twenty-Five

Positivity

Talking things up

'A positive attitude may not solve every problem but it makes solving any problem a more pleasant experience.'
Grant Fairley

If you can develop a positive attitude to life then you will be happy, because you will learn to see the best in everything you do and everyone you meet. But developing a positive attitude is incredibly hard for some people. To develop such a positive attitude you have to, as this book has been consistently telling you, learn to understand yourself and to know what is important in life. Too many people are searching for things in life that do not exist. Some people always want more and this leads to disappointment and to suffering. A simple starting point to developing a positive outlook on life is to set yourself realistic targets that are achievable.

Story

Sir Clive Woodward, the World Cup winning England rugby coach, tells a very good story about

Positivity

how he developed a very positive winning mind-set in his England team. More of this later, but one story he tells is about being very positive about everything you do and paying positive attention to even the smallest detail.

Jason Robinson, the England winger, when Clive Woodward took over as coach of England, was regularly getting stopped on his fleeting runs. Robinson had the ability to go flying past anyone but Clive noticed that the opposition were mainly stopping him by grabbing hold of his Rugby shirt collar. With a very positive attitude Clive Woodward worked with the shirt manufacturers to design a shirt that could not be grabbed so easily. This shirt worked, with England winning the World Cup.

Stimulus:

You can achieve anything in life, individually or as part of a group, team or larger organisation, if you develop a positive mind-set. There are many ways of doing this, although the approach used by Sir Clive Woodward seems to make a lot of sense and was very successful: Promote and develop five ways of being:

- *Enjoyment*. Enjoyment defined as belonging to a challenging environment in which everyone thrives. Ask yourself a question:

How many of your colleagues enjoy working with you?

- <u>*Lateral and vertical thinking.*</u> Re-write the rules, there are no rules, think differently, find the approaches that no one else has thought of. But, with all this lateral thinking don't forget the detail, vertical thinking, make sure that everything is done well. Question everything you do. There is nothing wrong with throwing everything out and just putting the things back in that you really want, but make sure you have covered all the angles.
- <u>*Critical non-essentials.*</u> Pay attention to the things that are not obviously important but, in fact, are essential to success. *What are the things that will set you or your organisation apart from the others?*
- <u>*Critical essentials*</u>. Pay attention to the core components – people, management and leadership. You need to develop a winning profile in yourself and in others. There are three components to the winning profile, the first two can be taught or coached, **1.** *skill* (talent), **2.** *leadership* (the ability to think correctly under pressure), **3.** *X-factor* (natural winner).
- <u>*No compromise*</u>. Whatever you are going to do, do it well – you can't cut corners.

Positivity

Advice:

Positivity is about developing a positive mind-set. The key is to live life the way you want to live it. **WANT** is the important word in this sentence. To do something well and to be truly positive about something then you need to **WANT** to do something. Live life by the rules you **WANT** to live by, not by other people's rules. There is a problem with this approach of course. That is, if you live by your own rules you also have to suffer the consequences. So the key advice is:

- Know who you are
- Know what you want
- Live by your own rules
- Take responsibility for your own destiny and your own actions
- Treat others as you would wish to be treated yourself
- Plan, plan and plan
- Make things happen
- Don't be knocked off course.
- Enjoy your life.

Action Point:

Count how many people at your work place actually like working with you. Be honest. Look at how they react to you, how they treat you, how happy they look when with you. *Are you creating positive vibes?*

Steve Kenning

Inspiration:

- **Sir Clive Woodward.** I heard him speak at a conference recently and he was incredibly inspiring. His positivity emanated around 1,700 people. Awesome!

Chapter Twenty-Six

Stress

This word really annoys me!

'Would you like me to give you a formula for success? It's quite simple, really. Double your rate of failure. You're thinking of failure as the enemy of success. But it isn't at all. You can be discouraged by failure - or you can learn from it. So go ahead and make mistakes. Make all you can. Because, remember that's where you'll find success.'

Thomas J. Watson

Stress is a word everyone understands and most people abuse. Some people are under tremendous stress in their personal or work lives, but many people simply use the word to describe their unhappy or difficult life. Most people can beat stress by taking control of their life and removing the things that they don't like or are giving them trouble. 'Impossible', I can hear you say, 'I couldn't do that.' *Why not?* If something is making you so unhappy and possibly unwell then remove the problem – you only live once.

Steve Kenning

Story

In my job I come across a great many people who are 'stressed'. Every one of them blames their stress on the job. In my organisation, where we do work people hard in a challenging and supportive environment, I know because we investigate each 'stress' case, that everyone who is stressed is so as a result of other things in their life. This might not be the case in every organisation but in my experience probably about 90%, a very arbitrary figure, of stress is not work induced. Here are a few examples from people I have worked with over the years:

- **Mrs X** – *spent all the time complaining that nothing was ever done right unless she did it herself and that the pressure this put her under was intolerable. Reality: Her marriage was a deeply unhappy one with a husband who belittled and undermined her. At work she was always looking to put others down in order to raise her self-esteem.*
- **Miss Y** – *always complaining about her workload. It turned out that she had a very serious illness and was wiped out after a few hours work and relied for the most part on painkillers.*
- **Mr B** – *was underperforming in his role and complained that the pressure senior staff were putting him under was unjust and stressful. This guy actually achieved*

Positivity

what he wanted, which was early retirement through stress related ill-health. However, I was a friend of his and he confided that he was stressed out though a new business venture he had set up on the continent that involved a lot of travel and risk. He wanted to retire, with all the benefits, to continue with his new career.

For each of these examples there are twenty more. There are very few instances where work does create stress in someone, for the simple reason that if the job is that bad **change it!**

However, stress can be caused by personal circumstances, ill-health or bereavement. This is a much more difficult thing to cope with. If you generally have a positive outlook on life the chances are you will find a positive way to deal with any situation.

Stimulus:

For every person who says that nothing can be done about a stress causing situation, there is someone who has done something about such a situation. In fact very positive people live their lives very differently to stressed-out people. Positive people see things differently and react differently and, as a result, are less stressed. There is a great deal of research about stress and how to reduce it.

Brian Farragher of the University of Manchester, recently commented that ambitious people who look to the future and don't dwell on the past are the least likely to suffer from stress. It is the people who are very goal-orientated, called the *'future'* group, who are best able to shrug off stress. The most stressed people were the *'past negatives'* who dwelt on past traumas.

Advice:

'For me my work is my life, the two are intertwined.'

Sahar Hashemi (founder of the Coffee Republic)

We spend 75% of our life at work, so you really need to get it sorted if it isn't working for you.

Action Point:

If you are stressed at this moment in time, try this.

Look at what is causing the stress. *Is it something at work, money problems, health, relationships?* Strip the situation down in your mind into all its different parts. Throw all parts away, send them out of your mind. Now just bring back the parts that you want. Build around the things that you

Positivity

want – add new things or ways of doing things to replace those you removed.

Whatever the result, it will have helped you to analyse the issue.

However, nothing will help if you are not honest about yourself, your issues and personality.

Inspiration:

- **Nelson Mandela** – after the life he has had to endure, he is surely someone we should all aspire to in relation to stress management.

Chapter Twenty-Seven

Heroes

Clint Eastwood!

'The secret of the man who is universally interesting is that he is universally interested.'

William Dean Howells

What is a hero? Someone who acts and behaves in a way that is inspirational to you. A hero is someone whose actions you may want to copy.

We are all heroes to a degree. We can all be heroes. Often we are heroes without even knowing it. We influence a whole range of people in a wide range of ways.

Story

We are all influenced by other people. We shape the way we look and the way we act by observing the actions of others. Clint Eastwood was always a real hero of mine. He was cool and said little but it was the wrinkles around his eyes that really impressed me. I spent the next few years squinting and smiling, trying to develop those wrinkles. At the time it didn't work, but some twenty years later – success!

Positivity

As you move through life there are certain people, and in particular things people say, that leave an impact on you. Such people are real heroes.

When I was sixteen, a friend and I were both very keen to leave school, get a job and enjoy the money. We were both in the top sets and quite capable of doing 'A' levels, yet we were very fed up with school. One day, Malcolm Birch, the Head of PE, sat us both down. We got on very well with Malcolm and we respected him. He told us how much we had to look forward to in life, but that we would be wasting the opportunities ahead of us if we didn't try to get the qualifications that would open up the future to us. He said we were too intelligent to get stuck in low level jobs and that we would regret it in a few years time. He told us about the glorious life of a university student and the attractions of the wider world outside of Stafford where we lived. Regardless of his efforts, we were both convinced that Malcolm wanted to keep us in school to maintain the quality of the school football, basketball and rugby teams, in which we were both integral players.

Malcolm's words lived with me for some time. I had a couple of interviews for jobs and, although I was offered them, I turned them both down and talked the school into letting me stay on, despite my very poor 'O' level results. My friend, Stuart, left and went to work for the council. Sixth Form was the best part of my school life. The only time I really enjoyed and the only time when I really worked at school. The A levels I gained helped me to eventually get a degree and then onto a really interesting job and a great lifestyle. Stuart, after a few years in his council job, really regretted leaving. After a few years he looked and behaved like a middle-aged man, he had lost his spark and seemingly, his youthful aspirations. Malcolm Birch was a hero to me, as his words changed my life.

Stimulus:

We should all strive to be heroes, but you can only be a true hero if you know and like yourself, because it is only then that you can be fully selfless to significantly support and influence other people.

True heroes know themselves so well that they don't use role models, instead they will look to develop themselves by observing the role actions of other people. A true hero knows that they are totally unique. They do not want to be just like other people. They know that no one is like them and they are like no one. They also know that they can develop themselves by taking the best actions of other people and adapting them into their own way of being.

Advice

Think carefully about the way you behave and the way you speak to people. Everyone is different and

Positivity

everyone is influenced by different things. This is exactly why you must be very careful of what you say and do.

Watch other people and identify the things that people do that would have an impact on your character if you adopted similar behaviour. We should all be looking to develop ourselves and people watching is one of the best ways to achieve this.

Action Point:

Behave like a hero for a day. Be fair, honest and open. Help and support other people. Put your interests on the backburner. Look to influence other people through the strength of your selfless actions.

Inspiration:

Clint Eastwood – Lines such as *'Do you feel lucky?'* and *'Make my day,'* the wrinkles, coolness, rugged good looks, acting and directorial talent, make him a hero to me!

Steve Kenning

Chapter Twenty-Eight

Creativity

There is always a better way

'Creativity is a central source of meaning in our lives.....when we are involved in it, we feel that we are living more fully than during the rest of life.'

Mihaly Csikszentmihalyi

Creativity is a wonderfully open word – it smacks of opportunity and 'anything goes.' Creativity is a word for the future. Western economies, no longer able to compete in the global labour market, will increasingly rely on the creativity of their people to maintain economic prosperity. Our education system however, with its increasing emphasis on testing and measurable results, is developing a generation that is fodder fed and unable to think for themselves. The exam system severely stifles creativity.

Story

A senior manager at a large multi-national engineering company in Telford once told me a story of the future. He told me about the changing nature of employment and the qualities that industry would need in the future.

Positivity

Ted, the senior manager, was relating to me an interview he had been involved in during the day. Things were not going too well at the company and they had been through a rationalisation programme to make the workforce leaner and more cost-effective. They had ensured that the younger workers were generally kept on. They were looking to the future. They had ten apprenticeships coming to an end and all were to be offered fulltime jobs. There was one key role that required precision skills and a high degree of engineering ability. Two of the apprentices had applied for this post. Dave, a very hard working apprentice, achieved the best results in his engineering qualifications, had the best attendance record, was very diligent and paid real attention to detail. The other candidate was Tom, a very good apprentice, with good results in his engineering qualifications, although his was sometimes a bit lax and often lost concentration, however, he always got the job done.

Ted asked me who I thought got the job. Obviously I thought totally reliable and hard working Dave. Ted agreed, saying that in every other case a Dave had got the job, however on this occasion Tom was given the post. Ted said that throughout the interview Dave was well ahead, until later, whilst discussing the candidates, one of the managers turned the qualities they were looking for on their head. He said that the company had been appointing Daves to jobs for years and, as a result, they were struggling. They made items of great quality but had lost their competitive edge. He said why not appoint Tom who was less hard working and liable to go off task, but he was very creative in his thinking. He would question their processes and designs and look for improvements. Everyone agreed and Tom was appointed.

So creative thinking on behalf of a manager led to the appointment of a creative worker. This conversation led me to think deeply about the kind of worker I was and the kind of workers I wanted working for me.

Stimulus:

- *Creativity* is about doing things differently, improving things, and looking at things afresh.
- *Creativity* takes you to where no one has been before.
- *Creativity* opens your mind and keeps you mentally alert.
- *Creativity* is available to everyone and can lead to a deeply satisfying existence.

Advice

The most enjoyable way to function in life at home or at work is to be one step ahead of everyone else. If you can see what's coming or shape your own

Positivity

future you get the benefit of being in control of your life. Creativity is about never being satisfied with the mundane, the inadequate, the inefficient and the complacent. Creativity is about finding the answer to your questions, inventing the future. The best advice is to question everything and find creative solutions to the things you do not like or want to improve.

Action Point:

Tomorrow morning think creatively about how you eat you breakfast. *Is there a different, more enjoyable way to eat it? Can your method be improved? For example, is warm milk on your frosties better than cold? Or is eating your toast chopped into lines of soldiers a more tasty approach than usual?*

If being creative works at breakfast time then what about taking the experiment further into other parts of your life?

Inspiration:

- **Madonna** – she is always reinventing her look and her *music*. A real creative genius.

Chapter Twenty-Nine

Sustaining Change

Keeping the ball rolling

'If you can give your son or daughter only one gift, let it be enthusiasm.'
Bruce Barton

In most jobs today you have to be prepared for change and to be able to handle it. Increasingly, if you want to be successful at work and in your personal life you have got to also be able to introduce and sustain change. *The occasional good idea is fine but how do you keep your organisation and your life consistently moving forward?*

Story

Once upon a time there was this great leader called Sir David. He had spent several years establishing himself in the area and he was well respected. He had a dream of creating the best castle in the country. So he researched the best possible designs, shopped for the best materials, employed the best designers and builders and had lots of innovative ideas and features put into his castle. As he built the castle people travelled for miles to marvel at this, probably the best castle in the land.

Positivity

For a couple of years David was solely focused on this project and by the time the castle was completed it was certainly the best castle in the country.

Sir David enjoyed the reputation he had acquired and he invited many people to visit him over the coming years to share in his creation. He was so busy basking in his own success that he became very complacent. He knew his castle was the best so why should he continue to look outside, he had achieved his vision, now was the time to enjoy it. Sir David did not notice or care that people were taking his ideas and designs and developing them, and soon word got out that there were even better castles than Sir David's and gradually people stopped coming to Sir David's castle. By the time Sir David realized what was going on it was too late – he had lost the competitive edge.

Stimulus:

The key to sustaining change is to never develop the mind-set that you've finally arrived, and that you have reached your vision. The trick is to reach your current vision then adjust it further. Sir Alec Ferguson, the manager of Manchester United, is a classic example of someone who has successfully sustained change. Manchester United has been at the top of the English game for many years. He has *achieved* this by constantly adjusting his vision and always looking to improve. When United won the

Steve Kenning

European Champions Cup Sir Alec celebrated for about five minutes and then immediately said he wanted to win it more times than any other English club.

Advice

Starting point

- Involve everyone in self-analysis and in building the new vision.
- Talk to everyone, make things happen for everyone, leave no-one untouched.

Make things happen

- Sell the vision - talk it, the people, and the organisation up.
- Get some successes.
- Identify and give responsibility to key people.
- Decide on your tools and agents for change - invest heavily (time and commitment).
- Sort out the culture (ideas, risks, responsibility, trust, etc).
- Introduce lots of things in order to reach the vision (but keep an eye on everything and talk people through difficulties).

Positivity

Keep on moving on

- Keep moving forward - don't wait to evaluate, keep looking outside, keep modifying the vision and build capacity and systems that support change.

Action Point:

This might sound impossible but try it! Choose one day and do everything differently to the way you usually do things. For example, put the alarm clock on the other side of the bed, eat your breakfast before your shower, drive your car on the wrong side of the road!!! *Perhaps not the last suggestion.* Try it – you might break out of your usual complacency!

Inspiration:

- **Not Marks and Spencer** – the company that was a household name and everyone's favourite department store is a prime example of how not to sustain change, of becoming too complacent and losing their market. (Although new management now seem to be reversing the decline!).

Chapter Thirty

Using your brain

Think, think, think

'Anyone can be clever, the trick is not to think the other guy is stupid.'

Jose Mourinho

The brain is a much underrated and under utilised organ. Considering that we are fairly advanced life form, or so we believe, it is incredible how many human beings do not appear to be able to control the workings of their brain. Not only do we regularly fail to think about what we are doing and why we do things, we also fail to look after, to feed and exercise, our brains. There is a growing awareness of the brain, both in how it works and how we can make the most of it, but despite this, we still do not instinctively utilise the brain to its best advantage.

Story

One of the cleverest people I have ever met was a teacher called John Luke. John was a bit of a maverick and not universally liked, mainly because he was fairly uncompromising and did his own

Positivity

thing. John had scraped into teacher training college and mainly taught rural science to the kids no one really wanted to teach. He loved the outdoors, was a mountain leader and regularly ran outdoor activity trips for children.

The main feature of John was that he was always happy, always active and always on the go. Nobody controlled him and he lived his life as he wanted to live it. There was nothing that phased him, nothing he felt he couldn't do. He could also hold a conversation with anyone about virtually anything.

John was this kind of person because he used his brain. He thought carefully about everything he did. He would not jump into anything until he had a plan of action. From this kind of approach to living he had realised that he could do anything and this had built his confidence greatly. John used to think, think and think again.

Stimulus:

The cleverest people are not necessarily the people who society considers to be the cleverest. These tend to be people with the highest level and best qualifications. These people are undoubtedly clever – clever at playing the exam game, clever at studying and remembering knowledge, clever at applying their knowledge. However, such people are sometimes one dimensional – clever in one particular area. If, on the other hand, you are someone who utilises their brain in a wide range of ways, is multi-skilled and able to think through any situation then you are surely clever. Such people use their brains to the full.

From Father Ted:

Dougal: **'What's going on?'**
Priest: **'I think Ted has a plan.'**
Dougal: **'No, I mean in general.'**

Back in the Renaissance period, Erasmus, the Dutch writer, scholar, and humanist, was reputed to be the last person who knew everything worth knowing. Since his time, knowledge has increased at such a rate that it is no longer possible for one person to know everything worth knowing. Instead, we must depend on others to share knowledge with us, plus a host of other resources - ideas, leads, opportunities, creativity, political support, financial capital, goodwill, and so on. We need contributions from others if we are to get our jobs done, achieve our goals, and fulfill our missions in life. We live in a connected world, now more than ever before. The best performers in the future will be those who invest in and capitalize on the network of connections and resources, building powerful professional communities.

Positivity

Advice

Try to train your brain. Be aware of your thought patterns and make sure you listen to your thoughts. Before you do something unusual, not part of your normal routine, think carefully about what you are going to do and why you are doing it. Consider the options and consider the implications of what you are going to do. The key is to think as much as you can and to do fewer things instinctively.

Action Point:

Stop reading this book. Analyse at this moment what your brain is telling you. Start to listen to what your brain is doing.

Inspiration:

- **Blackadder** – particularly during the Elizabethan period. Rowan Atkinson's character was always thinking and plotting to stay ahead of the game or to find the next clever quip. Perhaps not an inspirationally nice character but someone with a quick mind that was well used.

Chapter Thirty-One

Look after yourself

You function more effectively with a healthy body and mind

'A man too busy to take care of his health is like a mechanic too busy to take care of his tools.'

Spanish proverb

Quite rightly we are becoming obsessed with health. Eating the right things and regular exercise is not only good for your health but it could save nations billions of pounds in reduced health care costs. Few people equate good health with a healthy mind. If you look after your brain, then there is a very good chance that your health will be good.

Few people understand that your brain needs exercise and it needs rest. A good night's sleep will restore the brain to full power, but you also need to stimulate the brain by bombarding it with interesting information. You can do this by having fun sightseeing, going to art galleries, surfing the net, window-shopping, etc.

Positivity

The body also needs to be exercised and rested. At least one-third of the population has been diagnosed with high blood pressure or levels at the high end of normal. An easy way to help reduce blood pressure is to regularly exercise. Vigorous exercise for up to twenty minutes at a time, at least three times a week, is the minimum required to keep your body in tune.

Then there is what you eat!

Story

I know lots of people who are overweight, I know lots of people who are very fit, but I know fewer people who are very fit both mentally and physically.

Stimulus:

'If taking vitamins doesn't keep you healthy enough, try more laughter: The most wasted of all days is that on which one has not laughed.'
Nicolas-Sebastien Chamfort

The key to looking after yourself mentally and physically is positivity. It is very unlikely that you can keep yourself in good shape if you don't have the right attitude.

If you know and understand yourself, if you are happy with who you are, then you will want to look after yourself physically. People eat for comfort, and people sometimes lose themselves in obsessive fitness programmes. If you like yourself and if you are happy with your life then you will want to look good, you will want to feel good and you will want to live a long time – so you look after yourself.

Advice

Be positive about who you are and what you have to offer the world. Remember, you are unique. There is no one else in the world like you, so you had better look after yourself. Eat sensibly, don't over indulge, exercise regularly and use your brain, drink lots of water, think about everything you do.

Action Point:

Exercise three times a week for at least twenty minutes at a time.

Read a book, do a crossword, play bridge, play a computer game, or something else several times a day to exercise your brain.

Eat sensibly.

Think positively about yourself.

Positivity

Inspiration:

- **Gary Lineker** – the former footballer and TV presenter. He always seems to be very positive about himself, his child had leukaemia and his family came through it, he learnt Japanese and Spanish when he played football abroad, and he obviously keeps himself fit.

Chapter Thirty-Two

Resilience

Keep on, keeping on!

'Our greatest glory is not in never falling, but in rising every time we fall.'
Confucius

Some people have resilience in the bucket full. Others have so little that even the smallest setback throws their life completely off course. Resilience is vital to developing a positive attitude to life. It is a little paradoxical in that if you are very positive you will find that you are very resilient and that you will need to be less resilient as you will be more in control of your life. Whereas if you are not very positive you will need to be far more resilient as there will be many situations where resilience is needed. The answer then is to develop your **positivity** and your resilience will develop accordingly.

Story

If you have ever met me you would probably agree that I am not everyone's idea of what a typical Headteacher should be like. Visualise in your mind a Headteacher. Now visualise someone you would least expect to be a Headteacher – the second

Positivity

image is very likely to be much closer to me than the first. I laugh a lot, I don't understand or use big words, I'm not intellectually challenging, fierceness doesn't equate with my character, and I am not at all stuffy. Also, I don't wear a gown, or boring suits, and I am not going bald (well only a little!). All through my life I have tried to be different, to rail against custom and to try to change the educational world. I have also always had the self-belief to know that whatever I do I will do it well.

This belief though was severely tested when I was applying for Headships. I had been a very successful teacher and a very good Deputy Headteacher, but being the sole person in charge of a school with the ability to shape the future of many young people was a different issue. I applied for about 40 different headships over a few years and I had several interviews. In every case I impressed the LEA officers and the Governors with my energy, enthusiasm and my ideas, but I also scared them to death. How would they control someone so headstrong and such a risk taker?

Each time I returned having been through two or three days of interviews, which were emotionally and physically draining, I had to cope with the positive people who told me to keep trying and I would make it eventually, the people who told me to just accept it and settle down to a life as a really good Deputy Head and this school isn't that bad anyway, and worst of all, there were one or two people who would simply say that they could never see me as a Headteacher so I might as well give up now! This final comment was particularly destructive. It was said to me, regularly, by someone who was very close to me at the time. She even told me I hadn't got a chance just before I went for an interview. I can now look back and understand that there were other reasons for this attitude but at the time I needed real resilience to keep going.

When you know that you can do something and that you have the capability, but others don't see it, and they try to bring you down to their level, you need real resilience to keep going after your dream. My resilience came from a self-belief that I could make a difference in the role. I had done a great deal to improve my present school as Deputy Head and I knew a great many poor Headteachers. I knew I could do a good job. This attitude kept me going.

This positive self-belief eventually worked when a free thinking group of Governors ignored the advice of the education authority officers and took a risk in appointing me. For the first couple of years as Head, even though I was doing a very good job, I didn't feel like a Head. I felt like an imposter. I would meet old friends who just couldn't believe that I was a Headteacher.

Resilience comes from a positive attitude about yourself and from knowing what you are capable of.

Positivity

Stimulus:

I consider myself to be quite lucky in the life I lead and the good health that I have. I meet many people who have terrible pressures to face in their everyday life. Some of these people manage these pressures magnificently and are truly resilient.

Life is not straightforward for anyone. We have to accept that change will happen and that our lives will be full of peaks and troughs. I touched on this issue in a previous chapter – in order to become very resilient you need to regularly challenge yourself. If you are constantly pushing at your limits, taking yourself outside your comfort zone, then you will develop the skills to manage difficult times. You will build up your resilience.

Advice

Don't get too comfortable with your life. Take risks, do the things you want to do, and stretch your comfort zones. Life is full of unexpected situations, prepare for them. Develop a positive state of mind. Tell yourself that you can cope with anything life throws at you. Don't listen to the negative people in your life. Get to know yourself, test yourself, learn about your capabilities.

Action Point:

The next time something happens to you that is slightly difficult and is perhaps a bit of a setback, use positive mind techniques to deal with it. Don't let the situation deteriorate and overwhelm you. Immediately think about the good points about the predicament and consider what positive *steps* you could take to change the situation. If this works for you then use it again and again.

Inspiration:

- **Anyone** who has fought through a debilitating illness and got their life back on track. My mother is a good example of this. She remains very positive about life despite being debilitated by arthritis.

Chapter Thirty-Three

Resourcefulness

There just has to be a better way

'Fall seven times, stand up eight.'

Some people in life are endlessly cheerful, and annoyingly positive. Nothing in life is a setback to these people, everything is an opportunity.

What these people have is an inate natural ability to find a better way. They are inherently resourceful. They will not let any setback hold them back. In fact they probably don't even recognise a situation as a setback.

'When faced with an obstacle, I generally managed to sidestep it by thinking on my feet rather than confronting it head on.'

Sir Clive Woodward

Story

On leaving school at eighteen, I worked for a year in the Commercial Union office in Plymouth. I was an 'A' level trainee. One of only a few posts

Steve Kenning

nationally to appear each year. I would be trained for greater things in the insurance industry. My parents were delighted. Their working class dream for their son of a safe, secure job for life, had been achieved.

After about a month of complete boredom, being given very menial tasks and then gradually being trained to do tasks that, to me, seemed inefficient and bureaucratic, I decided that I would in fact apply to University and perhaps become something like a journalist. I did apply, got a place, but decided to continue at Commercial Union for the rest of the year to make some money. Just after Christmas I told my bosses of my plans. One or two wished me well but the vast majority were horrified that I was throwing away such a good career. The best line I can remember, and one that still amuses me today, was said to me by one of the claims managers, Graham Kane. Graham was an annoying man, always sweating, always overly gratifying to his seniors and obviously quite dissatisfied with his lot. Despite all this he said that if I worked really hard and put in the hours then I could one day have a job like his! Aaaargggghhhhh!

As a result, many years later, this sketch from The Office, TV comedy series, really made me laugh:

Gareth: **'Who's been thinking of leaving?'**
Dawn: **'I have.'**

Positivity

G: 'Well that's just stupid, you've got a job here for life.'
D: 'Yeah, actually I don't want to spend my life answering phones in some crappy sub-branch paper merchants.'
G: 'Dawn, work hard enough, and you could be answering those phones in head office, or a better paper merchants.'

Stimulus:

Your own conditioning is a strange thing. Different situations, different people, different words and incidents all shape who you are. That is why we are all unique. Why certain things stay with you more than other things, no one knows.

I am very resourceful. I will always make things happen, particularly out of a difficult situation. Someone once, quite unkindly I feel, likened me to the spiv character you would always get in a Second World War prisoner of war camp movie. The character that could always come up with a pinstripe suit for an escape. I really don't see myself like this but I know I am resourceful.

My resourcefulness, I think, comes from a desire to be in control of my life and to not let anything beat me. I believe that you can achieve virtually anything that you want to. This might require a great amount of hard work and discomfort, but if you keep the end result in sight you can do it. I remember being quite politically active in my younger years and I was particularly influenced by certain political musicians. One band in particular, The Redskins, wrote a couple of really good songs. One line, 'Keep on, keeping on,' has lived with me. Whenever I need inspiration this line comes into my mind and makes me keep going.

Advice

Take control of your life. Do not let other people do things to you that you do not like. To take control of your life you have to:

- feel good about yourself
- be positive about your life
- know what you want out of life
- know yourself
- make things happen for yourself
- Don't rely on other people to make things happen for you

Do all this and you will be a happy, resourceful person.

Action Point:

Make one thing happen for yourself that does not *rely* on anyone else doing things for you.

Positivity

Inspiration:

- **Indiana Jones** – whatever the situation, whatever the risk, he can always find a way out and smile why he is doing it. Life is a challenge to be enjoyed.

Chapter Thirty-Four

Complete Control

Do what you want to do, when you want to do it, with whomever you want.

'We want our voices to be heard. We want control over our lives. This is a fundamental shift in social maturity that has been about five decades in the making....'
Soshana Zuboff
Prof of Business Administration,
Harvard, 2004
(I used this quote earlier but it is so true it needs to be highlighted again!)

In today's world you need control. If you want to be happy you need to be in control of your own life. You need to know where you are going and how you are going to get there. What you do not need are people telling you what to do and when to do it. This need for control is very evident in very young people today. If you took time to think about the daily life of a very young person, under 25 years of age (I'm 49 and still young!), you would soon realize that they face a bewildering number of choices and opportunities, ranging from which TV channel, in my day there were three, now there are

Positivity

hundreds, to which ringtone to use. For this reason the very young have to make real decisions and as a result they have a great deal of control over their lives. This expectation of *control* over their lives is leading to a lot of conflict with older people whose conditioning is very different. *Is there any wonder that very young people are finding it difficult to accept the behavioral expectations of older people running schools based on an educational system modeled on Victorian times?*

Story

This is not so much of a story as an observation.

An increasing amount of people are taking control of their lives by following a more unconventional lifestyle. People are looking at their quality of life instead of getting themselves hooked into a career or lifestyle that overwhelms and takes over their life. People are looking to live in nice places, happy to earn less and want to spend more time with the people they want to spend time with. This kind of lifestyle is not an easy option as you do need to be very creative in finding sources of income and living the life you want to live.

Stimulus:

If you are going to lead a positive, successful and happy life you need complete control. This is not to say that you don't care for other people or consider their needs, you must. But, what you need to do is live life on your terms and not in the shadow of someone else.

There is a real problem with the philosophy of being in complete control of your own life. The problem is that to be in complete control you also have to take complete responsibility for your actions and your life. You can blame no one else.

Advice

Control your thinking and you will control your actions.

'My belief is that personal freedom cannot grow beyond personal responsibility. The more people that learn to be fully accountable for their lives, the more freedom each of us can enjoy and the more fulfilling all of our lives will be.'
Reed Konsler

Know what you want, plan what you need to do to get it, and then work at it.

'A clear vision, backed by definite plans, gives you a tremendous feeling of confidence and personal power.'
Brian Tracy

Positivity

Complete control over your life, accepting the benefits and the responsibilities, will lead to great self-knowledge and satisfaction.

Action Point:

Look at your life, home and work. *Who is dictating your life? Is it you or it someone else?* If it is other people consider what you could do to reclaim your life. Then do it!

Inspiration:

- **Roy Keane** – the former Manchester United midfielder. I am not a great fan of the club or the player but I do admire his unrelenting attitude to his life. He has the highest standards, takes personal responsibility and leads from the front. The row he had with the Republic of Ireland management during a World Cup said a lot for his standards. He was used to the highest standards of care, support and training at Manchester United and he wasn't prepared to accept lower standards when representing his country. He wanted to be in control of his footballing performance but he couldn't be if the conditions were not right.

Chapter Thirty-Five

Don't take yourself so seriously

Lighten up

'Humour is by far the most significant activity of the human brain.'
Edward De Bono

An entertaining game to play when you are severely bored whilst waiting for a train in London, is to sit back and people watch. Look at the way people walk, their deportment. Look at the way they speak to other people. *What are they wearing? How do they use their mobile phones?* What you will notice, after only a few minutes, is that people fall into one of several types: people that are confident with the way they are, look and who know themselves; people who are so consumed with something else, like love, that they don't care; people who lack confidence and scuttle along anonymously; people who talk to themselves; people who are very strident; and people who take themselves far too seriously.

'Everytime you smile at someone, it is an action of love, a gift to that person, a beautiful thing.'
Mother Teresa

Positivity

Story

People who, on the whole think they are more important than they really are and take themselves too seriously:

- **Actors like Dustin Hoffman, who have to live a part in order to get into character – does this mean that in preparation for the recent voice-over he did, as a dog in an animated film, he ate dog biscuits.**
- **Newsreaders and TV presenters – good god! Why do these people consider themselves so important? If you know the answer please don't bother to tell me, life is too short.**
- **Amateur dramaticists – do they all really live their lives with a broom stuck up their bums?**
- **Anyone who belongs to a gentleman's club –** *is it because they think they are special?*
- **People on trains talking as loudly as possible into their mobile phones.**

Stimulus:

In this world there is not enough time, and nothing of enough importance, to think that you are the most important person in it. We are born, we live and we die. Life passes us by far too quickly. *Who is to say that the stockbroker is more important than the train driver, or the ticket collector is more important than the social worker?* No one can make that judgement. We all affect and influence people in our own ways. This is often to do with our job, but it is more likely to be because of our personality. Doctors should have a massive impact on other people and so should be important people, but I have met quite a number of doctors with the personality of an *empty walnut shell* and as a result have a zero effect on other people. *Why then do some people consider themselves to be so important?* The answer lies in a lack of self-esteem and self-confidence.

People who take themselves too seriously, who consider themselves to be more important than anyone else, who claim their time is valuable and who are rude and disdainful to anyone they consider to be their lesser, are basically sad, inadequate individuals.

Advice

If you are one of these sad, inadequate people who need to lighten up and take themselves less seriously then you are probably reading this at this moment very disdainfully, or you are perhaps not even aware of the fact that everyone else considers you to be an arrogant, self-obsessed loser.

Positivity

Action Point:

If you do not already take yourself too seriously just remember one thing - be careful never to take yourself too seriously.

If you are someone who takes yourself too seriously then you need to give yourself a serious talking to. Discover yourself, find out what you really want and modify your behaviour to get the best out of your life and to get the best out of other people.

Inspiration:

- **Jonathon Ross** – the TV host. Although I don't know the guy, he is probably a complete pain to be around, but he seems to be very genuine and takes the mickey out of himself quite a lot, which must be difficult to do if you are as popular and successful as he is.

Chapter Thirty-Six

Personal Mastery

The key to it all

'Personal mastery teaches us to choose. Choosing is a courageous act: picking the results and actions which you will make into your destiny.'

Peter Senge

The general recurring point made throughout this book is that you really need to understand yourself if you are ever going to lead a life that lives up to your own expectations. If you know yourself you are more likely to know what you want and how you can get it, you are more likely to understand and get on with other people better, and you are more likely to enjoy life.

Personal mastery is an exciting approach to life. You will never achieve complete personal mastery, but the fun is in trying to get there. If you think you have achieved personal mastery then you probably haven't, as people with a high level of personal mastery live in a continual learning mode. They never *'arrive'*.

Positivity

'People with a high level of personal mastery are acutely aware of their ignorance, their incompetence, their growth areas. And they are deeply self-confident. Paradoxical?'

Peter Senge – The Fifth Discipline

The End

Finally, here are ten principles that might help you to work towards becoming increasingly positive:

1. **Know yourself and constantly seek self-improvement.**
2. **Be actively interested in learning and be good at it.** As a leader at any level, you must know your role and be good at what you do.
3. **Focus on the individual** – care about and value everyone. Provide opportunities for all.
4. **Know the people in your life, grow the people in your life and be generative.**
5. **Get people working together without the issue of status getting in the way and encourage people to support the growth of others.**
6. **Provide vision, direction, and challenge**.
7. **Seek responsibility and take responsibility for your actions.** Search for ways to guide your life, other people and your organization to new heights. And when things go wrong, they will sooner or later, do not blame others. Analyze the

Positivity

situation, take corrective action, and move on to the next challenge.
8. **Keep yourself informed and communicate findings.**
9. **Set the example and set standards.** Be a good role model. People must not only hear what they are expected to do, but also see.
10. **Make things happen and ensure that things get done.**

Finally, just remember that life is for living. So go out and enjoy yourself.

Steve Kenning

About the author....

Steve Kenning

Headteacher of a large secondary school in Cornwall for the past eight years.

He has written two novels, both set in Barcelona, 'Barcelona Betrayal' and 'La Hermandad del Noveno Noviembre (The Brotherhood of the Ninth of November), and a self-management, personal growth book, 'Positivity – The art of personal mastery.'

He lives in Devon and in Barcelona.

www.barca-only.com

pensadores futuros

Positivity

Other books by Steve Kenning:

La Hermandad del Noveno Noviembre (The Brotherhood of the Ninth of November)

Published by Exposure Publishing in 2006
ISBN 1-84685-307-9

An extract from the thriller:

We looked at each other. We were scared and the tension, provided by Detective Ferran's lack of ability to protect us, filled the room. Eventually the detective spoke.
'You must realise that there is a lot of important information in this case. So far seven of the original twelve players in FC Llotja are dead, five have died in the last few days. This is a serious situation and one which is taxing the whole of the Mossos d' Esquadra.' He looked away from us and sipped at the water. He looked dreadful.
'I must tell you that we found evidence of recent visitors to the home of Jordi Torras. We do not think that he was alone when he died.'
'You think he was murdered?'
My mind was still racing.
'You know that we did not go inside his apartment....the old lady saw us outside.'

Steve Kenning

'You are not suspects....do not worry. However, his death may not be as straightforward as it first seemed.'

Available from Amazon.co.uk

Or from: www.barca-only.com

Positivity

Barcelona Betrayal

Published by Exposure Publishing in 2006
ISBN 1-84685-501-2

An extract from the thriller:

'Cracked her Ferran?' Roared Desanyo. Ferran hadn't seen him. He was surprised by his voice. Small, fat and annoying, with a brain similar in size and nature to that of a rodent, was how Ferran viewed the Detective. Desanyo was leaning back in his chair smiling. He could tell by Ferran's body language that he hadn't got anything from the woman. Another detective was sitting opposite him, mirroring Desanyo's actions. Ferran glanced at Martes. He really, really disliked this jumped-up excuse for a detective. Smarmy and unattractive, personality had totally bypassed this creature. He looked at his mouth. Martes was licking his lips. He had this habit of quickly licking his lips several times just before he made a wisecrack at someone else's expense. True to form, Martes joined in with the baiting.
'She's English isn't she? I would have thought with your blood you would have fucked her by now.' He jeered.
Ferran flipped. He hated the majority of the other male detectives at Gran Via. The young ones were OK, but the older ones were chauvinists, bigots and parochial. They were also pretty thick and corrupt, according to the book of Ferran. He felt

Steve Kenning

nothing but pure rage as he flew through the air towards Martes. It all happened so quickly. Perhaps it was because of the early hour, Ferran didn't normally wake fully until 10 a.m, and today it was not yet 7 a.m. Had he had time to take in what he was doing, he would have loved the shocked expression on the face of his fellow detective. Martes was nailed to his chair as he watched the six foot five inches of Ferran flying towards him through the air. The right foot of Ferran was stretched out in front of him as, almost in slow motion, his right heel smashed into the nose of Detective Martes. The impact was instant. Martes fell to the floor. The blood splattered everywhere. The flow and spray was immediate. As Ferran landed in a clump on the ground amidst a mess of office stationery, Martes was struggling to his feet, holding his broken nose trying to stem the flow of blood and the pain.

'You bastard, you have broken my nose. You bastard.' He ran away from the scene, trailing blood over all the paperwork and making a lot of noise. Desanyo looked on, stunned. He couldn't believe it. His body language showed that he wasn't going to take on this madman though. He sat still, looking at Ferran.

Available from Amazon.co.uk

Or from: www.barca-only.com

Printed in the United Kingdom
by Lightning Source UK Ltd.
116580UKS00001B/7-39